Slow Dying

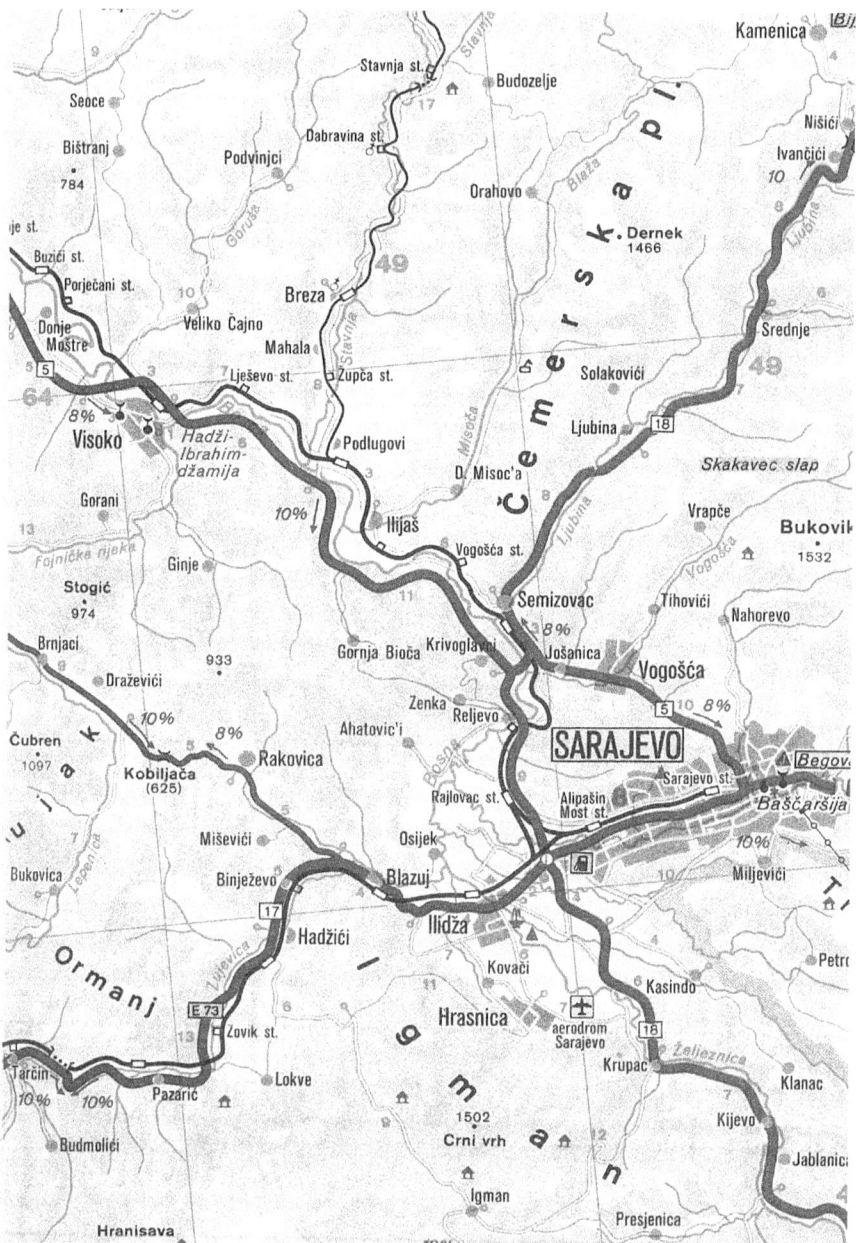

Slow Dying

The Bosnian War Prison Camp at Visoko
Diary and Testimonies

Fourth Edition

By Milenko S. Milanović
Originally edited by Dr. Momčilo Mitrović

✽ Brandylane

First Edition published August 1994, Military Publisher, Belgrade;
Second Edition, February 1995, Military Publisher, Belgrade;
Third Edition, April 2007, Beoknjiga, Belgrade

ISBN 978-0-9838264-4-6
Library of Congress Control Number: 2011944273

Brandylane Publishers, Inc.
www.brandylanepublishers.com

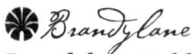

My uncle and I
Miloš and Milenko Milanović
(Photograph taken 1965)

To my uncle, Miloš Milanović (1933-1999), who inspired me to write this book. We were imprisoned in the war camp together.

Contents

Appendix

Preface to the First Edition, 1994

Visoko is a little Bosnian town, about thirty kilometers from Sarajevo, grown at the mouth of two rivers, Fojnica and Bosna, and the railroad Bosanski Šamac-Sarajevo. It has a history similar to many Bosnian and Herzegowian towns. The town-fortress Visoko is mentioned for the first time at the middle of the fourteenth century, when it had a strong trading colony and custom house at Dubrovnik. At the time of the medieval ascension there was a centre of Bosnian rulers, and as a king's town it had its own prince. It fell into Turkish hands in 1463 and stagnated for centuries. At the end of the nineteenth century with the building of a railway, Brod-Sarajevo began to develop trades, architecture and other industries.

Before the war, Visoko was a town of diverse citizenry, and they appeared to live harmoniously. In the municipality of Visoko, there were 46,130 citizens, among them 34,385 Muslims (74.8%), 7,377 Serbs (16%), 1,973 Croats (4.3%), 1,456 Yugoslavs (3.2%) and 939 others (2%).

Among the population were shadows of the past, especially the suffering of the Serbian nation during the Second World War. This was still alive among the Serbs who remembered the crimes that the *ustashas* had done to the Serbian people, especially to priests and other prominent, quiet citizens. There were still Serbs alive from Visoko who knew of the persecutions of Serbs in the prison camps in Caprag, Stara Gradiška and others. Many of them knew of the plunders of the Serbian properties, murders at home doorsteps, dead bodies in the river, and the refugees. They knew of the forbidden use of Serbian letters—*Cyrilic ALPHABET*—going out of all Serbian institutions. They knew the families of the executioners.

But there were no prison camps during the Second World War in these areas.

In the new war, Visoko would be remembered for the prison camp. It would join the long list of towns in which the pains and suffering of one nation beside another nation happened for one reason only: because the Serbs belonged to another nation and another religion.

This book preserves the diary by Milenko Milanović and the words of his companions from the prison camp. The testimonies and the diary display the whole picture about the struggle and suffering of Serbian people in Visoko.

The diary is dramatic testimonial proof about one human being's days of violent treatment and captivity. It identifies the life that was lived, the enmities and intolerances that brought violence and death. It captures the swirls of politics and ideology that can infiltrate the lives of an individual and make him a victim or an executioner. Time in the prison camp is noted from day to day and hour to hour. In addition to the daily pain and suffering, the diary entries address the pain of ideological viewpoints, political events and the painful loss and changes that the triple fall of Yugoslavia left behind (the fall of the socio-political system, the enmity between nations, and the fall of Yugoslavia as a state). The madness of exclusiveness, intolerance, and hatred of ruling powers was poured into the methodology of violence.

In the diary, the victims and executioners—past friends, school friends, neighbors, people with their visions, hopes, fears, inhibitions, suspicions, aspirations and aims—meet face to face in a diabolical conflict.

It is my special pleasure to thank Milenko Milanović for his courage to keep a diary in the face of such a threat.

Dr. Momčilo Mitrović, Organizer
Historian/Director of Institute for Serbian History

Publisher's Note to the Fourth Edition

Under extremely difficult conditions in the Visoko camp and in secrecy, author Milenko Milanović was able to write only brief diary entries. He later added comments and explanations to give his readers a clearer and more complete understanding of what happened. To avoid detracting from the power of the words as originally written in his diary, explanations added later are indented and put in brackets immediately following the diary entry to which they refer. After he was released, he expanded the entries, which were published in the Second Edition in 1994 in his native language.

This is the first edition in English, and includes both the original diary entries with explanations, as well as selected expanded entries.

Acknowledgements

When I left the prisoner-of-war camp and lived with my family, helpless and godless in a refugee camp in Serbia, Dr. Momčilo "Moco" Mitrović stepped up like an angel from heaven and helped me to find new hope—not just by editing and publishing the first edition of this book (Belgrade, 1994), but more so by helping me to believe again in people, in God and family. Moco, thanks for everything until the end of my life.

After many years of trying to publish this book in the US, with hundreds of rejections from different publishers, I finally found a publisher in Richmond, Virginia. Thanks to Robert Pruett and all of the others at Brandylane for their hard work.

Thanks to my parents for raising me and helping me to survive the P.O.W. camp, bringing me food and helping me keep my belief in God and in people. Thanks also for encouraging me to go as far as possible from Bosnia, because that is not my home any longer. God bless you.

I also would not be who I am without my family. Thanks to my wife Izabela for helping me through many sleepless nights because of my nightmares, and the many days of my depressive behavior and rudeness. I am sorry for that, Izabela. Thanks, and you know I still love you like the first day I saw you. Thanks to my kids Tamara and Ogi for hugging, kissing and consoling me without knowing why I was crying.

And thanks to everyone who helped me when I came to America and started a new life. Thanks to my soccer-playing friends, Michael, Shanc, Barnic and the others. Thanks to Jeff Sulik, a great man who is still helping refugees, and Patricia McInnis, a beautiful lady and person who helped me to get my house. Thanks to all my coworkers at Cadmus, but especially to my friends, Mike, Carl, Hank, Fred and Steve.

Without all of your love, support and encouragement, this book would not have been possible.

Introduction

To this day, the Balkan Wars are a chapter of history marked by deep controversy and confusion. Unlike World War II, the historical thrust of which has been largely agreed upon by all but the most radical historians, the wars that brought about the next acts of European genocide have yielded dissonant accounts. Historians, survivors and bystanders frequently disagree on matters of culpability, cause and motive. Whether the atrocities actually meet the definition of genocide, the roles of leading political and military figures, the characterization of the conflicts as international or civil wars, and even the gritty details of casualty reports have received much scrutiny and debate. Among others, the question of whether these were wars driven by longstanding ethnic tensions or the shrewd manipulation of the people by power-hungry leaders remains hotly contested.

In seeking to understand a subject so stripped of a clear, objective truth, the value of personal, subjective testimonies is ironically increased. For however they began, these were, in the end, tragically personal wars, waged within villages and homes, between neighbors and friends, and fueled by that most personal of inducements: fear. For those who survived, the fallout of the wars is less a matter of political change than the loss of the lives they led before the fighting started. This book is not an attempt to deal comprehensively with the Bosnian War; it is rather one man's story of suffering and survival in the face of suspended humanity. Still, to establish the setting of his experience, some preliminary—if perhaps not universally palatable—history is in order.

In 1991, the Socialist Federal Republic of Yugoslavia, for all intents and purposes, ceased to exist. In the wake of President Josip Broz Tito's death in 1980, the fragile balance attained during his nearly five decades in power collapsed, plunging Yugoslavia into years of economic and political instability. Across the republics, new leaders emerged, touting divergent and at times divisive ideologies. The republic of Serbia found a leader in the form of Slobodan Milošević, a man who would become a key and controversial figure in the upcoming years as he worked for what was and is viewed by some as the preservation of Yugoslavia, by others as the formation of a larger, stronger Serbia. As talk of a breakup increased, many Serbian Serbs began to fear what this would mean for ethnic Serbs living in other republics. Memories of Serbian genocide at the hands of Croatia during World War II ran close to the surface as Milošević and his followers postulated that should a breakup occur, Serbs living outside of Serbia would fall victim to persecution. Meanwhile the republics of Croatia and Slovenia found themselves increasingly swayed by the prospect of political independence and greater economic prosperity. By 1990, it was clear to many that Yugoslavia was poised to dissolve under a climate of growing uncertainty, paranoia and ethnic and nationalist tensions.

All of this came to a head on June 25, 1991, when Croatia and Slovenia declared their independence from the union. Milošević immediately dispatched a thousand troops to the Slovenian border, starting a ten-day war in an attempt to preserve unity; however, the small Slovenian army delivered a quick and unlikely victory against the stronger Yugoslav People's Army (JNA).

In retrospect, Milošević's critics argued that he'd had little intention of preventing Slovenia's secession. Small, geographically distant and without a sizeable Serbian population, Slovenia did not factor into what many have deemed Milošević's true vision in the wake of Yugoslavia's failure—a greater Serbia. Croatia, with its large Serb faction, would not get off so easy. Milošević's insistence that Serb-populated regions within Croatia remain a part of Yugoslavia was geographically complicated and unacceptable to Croatia. Thus, the Croatian War quickly followed and would leave 20,000 dead by the time the JNA withdrew the following year. Croatia won its independence, but the JNA was not defeated and pulled its weapons and resources with it into Serbia.

When the international community recognized Croatia's sovereignty in January of 1992, Bosnia-Herzegovina was left with limited options: follow suit and declare independence as well, or join what remained of Milošević's Yugoslavia. Having witnessed the JNA's inability to defeat Croatia, and loathe to become part of what he deemed Greater Serbia, Bosnian president Alija Izetbegović chose secession despite the popular opposition of Bosnia's Serbs, who owned 59% of the land. Thus began the bloodiest conflict to take place on European soil since World War II.

The Bosnian War stretched from April of 1992 to December of 1995 and resulted in all manner of atrocity. Made up of Muslim Bosniaks, Serbs and Croats, the population of Bosnia was deeply ethnically divided, rendering the climate ripe for catastrophe in a nationalist war. Meanwhile, Croatia had staked its own claim to Bosnia's Croatian regions and moved in as well, brutally fighting both Serbs and Muslims for territorial control. Three opposing armies were formed within Bosnia: the Muslim Army of the Republic of Bosnia and Herzegovina (Army of BiH), the Croatian Defense Council (HVO), and the Serbian Army of Republika Srpska. Former neighbors, colleagues and friends suddenly became enemies based on nationality. Prison camps sprung up in newly conquered territories, and reports of ethnic cleansing and mass graves abounded. By war's end, all three sides were guilty of ethnic cleansing.

In what has been widely regarded a grave failure of the West, neither the U.S. nor the U.N. dispatched troops to end the fighting. After more than three years of fighting, NATO intervened in August of 1995, and a few months later, peace negotiations were finalized with the signing of the Dayton Agreement. Bosnia-Herzegovina was divided into two separate parts—the Serb Republic, with 49% of the land, and the Muslim-Croatian Union, with 51% of land, as it stands today—and joined Croatia, Slovenia and the peacefully liberated Macedonia as independent states. By that time tens of thousands had been killed and more than a million displaced.

Through it all, the role of the media in the Balkan wars and the ensuing confusion can hardly be overstated. In Serbia and Croatia, television, radio and print incurred acute government censorship and compelling propaganda, and independent media was suppressed. Serbian fears of their brethren falling victim to violence were fanned with true reports of Serbs fired from their jobs in Croatia and Bosnia, along with emotional appeals to the Serbs' history of persecution. Nationalism was the popular rhetoric of the media in both Serbia and Croatia, such that members of both sides believed they were fighting in the name of self-preservation of their nation and its rights.

In Bosnia, the official media often reported only one side of the conflicts, and to this day, speculation persists that the Bosnian government may have orchestrated violence to draw media attention to their cause. One of the bloodiest and most highly publicized events of the war, the 1994 Markale massacre in Sarajevo, is still swathed in mystery, believed by some to be an instance of the Bosnian government shelling its own people and blaming Serbs in order to garner sympathy and drag Western powers into the war.

In the Western world, the media was similarly selective. In Western Europe and the U.S., the story of the war was one of Serbian aggression fueled by longstanding ethnic hatred. Daily, the Western world witnessed the Serbs, and to a lesser extent, the Croats, engaged in acts of invasion and ethnic cleansing against the Muslim Bosniaks; but the ethnic cleansing of Serbs by Muslims was largely ignored. Little attention was given to violence inflicted on Serbs, or to the Serbs in Serbia, Bosnia and Croatia who resisted or were the casualties of this powerful tide of aggression and corruption. The anti-war efforts of Serbian citizens and independent media; the thousands of Serbian Serbs who fled rather than fight a fratricidal war; the Bosnian Serbs who risked their lives to protect their Muslim neighbors; and the Bosnian Serbs who refused to leave their homes and who themselves fell victim to acts of brutality at the hands of the Croatian and Muslim armies, were not widely publicized.

In the Balkans, incendiary reporting and propaganda contributed to the inflamed tensions and sense of victimization and national destiny that led peacefully coexisting people to turn against one another. In the rest of the world, a simplified narrative of war has contributed to longstanding anti-Serbian sentiments, fueling the characterization of Serbs as a bellicose and brutal people. It's a stereotype *Slow Dying's* author, Milenko Milanović, has lived with for years.

When he was at last freed from eight months of harsh internment in a Bosnian Muslim war camp just miles from his home, Milenko began his new life as a Serb refugee in Serbia. He carried with him loose-leaf pages of a journal detailing his experience, carefully hidden in the lining of his jacket. Over the next few years he would set about expanding these hastily scrawled notes into book form, which was subsequently published in Serbia. Then, in March 1995, Milenko and his family immigrated to the U.S., and he embarked on a new challenge: getting the book published in America in an effort to balance perceptions of the Bosnian War and give voice to the plight of Bosnian Serb civilians who were caught in the conflict. This book—a marriage of his original journal with the written testimonies of his fellow prisoners—is the culmination of those efforts.

Perhaps it should come as no surprise that a singular truth is so elusive in the history of the Balkan Wars. They were wars waged by multiple sides for complex and various aims, and inevitably, what little clarity there was at the start quickly devolved into the terrifying corruption that is borne of fear, desperation and isolated power in the suspension of order and reason. Human kind was not built to go to war and come out unchanged. By some miracle, the strongest participants maintain their humanity; others lose themselves in the chaos. In the end, everyone left standing staggers away to deal with the ghosts of war. The 19th century philosopher Bertrand Russell famously said, "War does not determine who is right—only who is left." Milenko Milanović and the others who contributed to this book are some of the people who are left. *Slow Dying* is their story.

Editors, Fourth Edition

The Dreams!

The water was so calm and clear that from the boat I was able to see the fish, which, with slow movements of their fins, often changed the direction of their swimming. To me, their twitching and spinning looked like a game. They swam around the bait on my fishing hook, gently touching it with their mouths, pushing it left and right, not even thinking to snap at it and be caught. It was as if they were playing, just like careless children somewhere on a meadow full of flowers. At first their game amused me, but gradually I began to lose my patience. The spring sun was beginning to show itself above the treetops on a nearby hill, lighting up the calm surface of the water and letting me know that fishing was over for that day. With slow strokes, I set off to the shore. The caught fish were still wiggling in the net that hung on the boat.

All of a sudden, as if someone blocked the sunrays with their hand, everything grew dark. The huge dark clouds, which carried rain, appeared from nowhere and covered the sky with horrible thunder and lightning. I was rowing faster and faster, but the shore seemed farther and farther away. It was raining so heavily that I was not able to recognize the surface of the water of the lake, which had been so calm just a few minutes earlier. Between two hills I could see a swollen brook, which was rising higher and higher as it flew into the lake. The muddy mountain water was filling the lake, making huge waves, which were carrying me somewhere. In that muddy water it was as if I saw my mother, father, relatives, neighbors . . . Suddenly, the lake seemed to open up with a horrible explosion, and I felt myself falling into the abyss. I screamed as loudly as I could . . .

When I opened my eyes, I saw the bedroom window lit by the same sun I had seen in the dream. The sound of the explosion was still echoing in my ears as I thought about how a beautiful dream had ended so badly. I also remembered the horrible muddy water and wondered whether there was any symbolism in it. I looked at the clock: 6:30 a.m. On the calendar it was June 20, 1992. I didn't even think about falling asleep again. I was a little bit dizzy, which, I believed, could be relieved by strong morning coffee. After a shower, I drank my coffee and thought about my wife and daughters who, almost a month before, had left to visit my sister in Berlin because of the war danger in Bosnia. I looked at their photographs, wondering whether they had changed in the past month. I missed them so much, and the house was empty without them. The sound of an explosion roused me from my thoughts. I wasn't sure whether it was an echo from the dream or reality. Only when I heard the burst of machine-gun and rifle fire did I realize what was going on. *So the war has knocked on our door, too,* I thought. Not even this beautiful valley, where I had spent the best days of my life, would be spared the whirlwind of war which was going on so close, and yet so far away, on the border of the municipalities Visoko and Ilijaš, only ten kilometers from my home.

I thought about my father and mother, who lived in the neighboring settlement, and I shuddered. Were they alive? As if in a delirium I took a gun and ran towards their house. The rifle fire had not ceased, and the bullets buzzed around me like bees and cut the young corn stalks. Everything was swarming like a beehive. I heard a detonation, one, two, three . . . somewhere nearby. At one moment I felt as if I was flying and then falling, falling . . . The taste of the earth and the smell of the grass woke me from sleep. I lifted my head, and in the distance I saw all those faces I had seen in the muddy water of my dream. My mother and father, with their hands tied with wire, together with the others, were being escorted by soldiers in an unknown direction. I was not able to move, and I wanted to help them, to bring them back. The cocking of a rifle behind my back roused me again and it began to roar in my ears. I managed to shout, "Mother, Father . . . !" And then the black hole opened, and I fell into it . . . I screamed!

The Time Being . . .

Someone was shaking and jolting me, and I didn't know whether I was dead or alive.

"Wake up, wake up, that was just a dream," someone said. When I finally opened my eyes, I saw my wife Izabela's worried face. Wiping away the tears that were running down my face, she told me in a soothing voice, "You had nightmares and bad dreams again."

I was shaking and crying. I didn't know if it was because of the fear, or because I was happy I had awakened. I wondered if this was still a dream.

"Don't worry. Everything is over," she said. "The things that happened to you will never happen again, especially not here in America. I'll go and make some coffee for you while you take a shower. You have to go to work soon," she said on her way out of the room.

I replaced my pillow, which was wet from tears and sweat, with hers. I was left by myself in the room, thinking. Dear God, weren't ten years enough to forget everything that was bad? Didn't I suffer and lose enough in my life, and wasn't it time that I at least slept like a normal man? What was this thing that had been pressed so deeply into my mind, and which could not be removed for good? I thought, *I have been in America for ten years already, and I still dream about what happened. I am still fighting, running away, falling, getting up and falling down again, and always at the end that damned black hole and the scream. Everything is the same, over and over again. Is there an end to it, and what's waiting for me tomorrow?* The pictures from my recent past began to show in front of my eyes.

When the American consul in Belgrade approved my departure to America, and after the checkups and tests were done, I was the happiest man in the world. At last my life as a refugee in Serbia had come to an end and I would be able to start a new life with my family. I wanted to run away to anywhere, away from my never forgotten Yugoslavia, where the war was blazing now. I was born there, I had a happy childhood and a very happy life there, until the war started and destroyed everything that once had been so nice. It was a strange feeling to run away from something you once loved and now hated. My Yugoslavia, the old one before they started to separate it into Republics, will always be a part of me and something most beautiful in my heart. I will always be a Yugoslav, and never a Bosnian, which I would be according to the new Republic affiliation. When that damned, fucking Bosnia was founded, I and my future life disappeared, and my past also disappeared, because they plundered and took everything I had ever had. And in the end, I was a refugee.

Thirsty and hungry, dirty and miserable, but still proud in my heart, I was accepted into America to start a new life. Although I knew a lot about America, I had never thought of living there. We had to learn about it for school, starting from Columbus, and moving on through the Wild West and Indians, Cochise, David Crockett and the Alamo, the Civil War, Lee and Grant, Nikola Tesla and the Niagra Falls, JFK (who was my grandfather's favorite president) and Marilyn Monroe, Vlade Divac and the NBA, Monica Seles and so on and so on.

We left for America towards the end of winter of 1995. The few clothes we had as refugees fit into two suitcases, even though there were six of us: my wife, three children, my mother-in-law and me. We went from Belgrade to Budapest, Hungary, by bus and from there flew to New York because the flights from Belgrade had been cancelled due to the sanctions. The journey and the necessary documents were supplied by the International Organization for Migration (IOM) in Belgrade. When we set off from Belgrade, my relative Gordana Dragić saw us off and gave me Serbian-English dictionaries with the remark that I would definitely need them. She then wished us a happy new life in America.

When we landed in New York, the song "New York, New York" played quietly from the speakers, and I thought about the life that was waiting for me. There were many new things: I was about to encounter the English language for the first time, and there would be no real opportunity to use the French and German my wife and I had learned. I would have my first encounter with black people in my life. I would also encounter cockroaches in the miserable apartments where we were lodged, Food Stamp living and medical examinations with the many protective injections we would receive so as not to infect America, as if we'd come from Africa and not from civilized Europe.

The six of us settled into a two-room apartment south of Richmond on Remuda St. It was more than miserable. Besides three mattresses on the floor, there was nothing else in the bedroom. In the living room there was a sofa, a little wooden table and three chairs. A lot of time passed before we had our first meal sitting all together at the same table. Our neighbors were Vietnamese, Cambodians, Africans and Bosnians, so I wasn't even sure where I was. The only proof that I was in America was the English language on our television, which someone had given us and which looked more like a piece of furniture than a television set. Several years later, I bought another set just like it at a yard sale for fifteen dollars, as a reminder of the times when my children had sat and listened to TV quietly, since if they ran about the room the TV would lose reception and the picture would disappear. If we wanted to watch something, we all had to gawk at the TV, almost without breathing. We only watched, and could understand nothing. I don't know why, but we watched the cartoons most often. I was so disappointed about America that I was lucky I had no money to buy tickets to return to Serbia, because I would have certainly done so. I also had to incur more than $7,000 in debt for the tickets to come to the United States, therefore starting my new life in debt.

The clerk, who worked for Richmond Immigration Services, was from Yugoslavia. She tried to find us jobs as quickly as possible, no matter the kind, so as to get rid of us, so that they wouldn't have to give us food stamps and insurance any longer. That's how, after two months, I was employed as a sorter of waste materials for Recycle America. I lost food stamps before I had received my first paycheck. I immediately lost social insurance, which my company did not provide for the first three months, so in that period we lived on chance. My mother-in-law also lost her insurance, and for the next three years we prayed to God that she didn't become ill, and if she did, that she would die quickly, since we didn't have enough money for hospital bills. Fortunately, after three years she earned the right to insurance through Henrico County, because she was sixty-two years old. You can do anything in America except be ill.

Curiously enough, I learned very quickly how to work in recycling. I immediately learned the difference between plastic and glass bottles, brown, green and clear glass, gallons for milk and bottles from Coca-Cola. I even learned how to drive a forklift. Since I was working with other refugees, my English did not improve a bit. The only help I had was Jeff Sulik, who voluntarily organized the school for English in the settlement where I lived. He was the only ray of hope that I would ever learn English.

The days passed. My wife worked as a cleaner in the Hotel Marriott, and I prayed to God to have more overtime hours and to earn as much as possible. Before coming to the USA, Izabela had worked as medical lab technologist in a military hospital in Sarajevo, which was the best hospital in Bosnia and Herzegovina. The fight for life continued. Checks, bills, days and months rushed by like on a film tape, and we managed to survive. Thanks to playing football for Cosmos, the team which my two relatives Siniša and Jovan (who came to Richmond six months before me) played for as well, I met new people and made new friends.

In 1996 I moved to Royal Homes to work as a supervisor for a roofing company. During my everyday work I visited Richmond and its surroundings, and after that the whole state of Virginia as well. I got to know its beauties, and the idea of staying there became more and more pleasant to me. I thought about my country less and less often. The only thing I missed were my parents, who are so far away. I didn't improve my knowledge of the English language through this work either, since all the other workers were Hispanic and spoke Spanish.

The following year, 1997, my supervisor from recycling called me to go and work at AFGD Glass Co. as an oven operator for higher wages. Unfortunately, there the workforce was the same as before, and my English still did not improve, except for the slang, which I mastered well. When I left the company the following year, 90% of the workers were Bosnians.

In August 1998, I started working in a printing firm called Cadmus, and from that year on, I can say that my family and I started living a fairly good life. I was employed in a stable company with the prospect of learning and progressing in my knowledge of the language. My wife at last got a job at the Virginia Institute for Cancer as a laboratory technician, which was work she did in Yugoslavia. My children were excellent at school and they had no problems. With a help of Patricia McInnis, the wife of my friend Michael, we bought a house in Henrico County where there were excellent schools. Finally, I got in touch with my parents, who lived in Bosnia, and everything was getting better.

Everything but those damned dreams of mine, which haunted me at night. I tried to get rid of them in various ways, but they would come again after a few days . . .

"The coffee is on the table, come down quickly or it will get cold." The voice of Izabela, who didn't know that I was still in bed, roused me from my thoughts. I quickly got dressed and ran down the stairs to the living room.

The coffee will refresh me well, I thought.

When Izabela saw me with mussed-up and wet hair, unshaven and without clothes for work, she asked, "What have you been doing when you didn't have a shower and you didn't shave?"

"I have been thinking," I answered coldly.

"And . . . have you thought it over? You have been thinking for ten years, and everything is the same and nothing changes. Neither talks nor teas, nor the strongest sleeping pills have helped you. The only thing that helps you is Jack Daniels when you get drunk. You fall asleep like a baby." Almost like automatic fire, my wife attacked me.

"Better anything than nothing," I again replied coldly, drinking warm coffee, the taste of which put me in a good mood.

Then, in a more gentle tone, she told me, "I am not

attacking you because of myself. Don't you see what you are doing to yourself? I think it's high time you asked help from a psychologist. Let him examine you and determine where all those things come from and let him help you with some therapy. They have the most modern devices here, the best pills, and I think that there must be some help for you. I beg you to promise me that you will go and see a psychologist. Promise me," she said.

She hugged me gently and kissed me with an encouraging smile, knowing that I didn't like to go to the doctor, especially not a psychologist. He couldn't possibly know what was in my head better than me, and he couldn't tell me what to do in order to get well. I vaguely recalled the words I used to say: *If someone goes to see a psychologist, he is a fool.* Of course I had to promise her that I would go.

We continued drinking coffee and talking about our plans for the following days, when I heard a roar on the stairs from Tamara and Ognjen (nicknamed Ogi), who were running downstairs to kiss us before they started getting ready for school. Ogi, my youngest son, arrived first and he simply jumped onto my knees, almost spilling the coffee.

"You see, I am faster than Tamara," he said, hugging me.

"If you are, that's only because I let you," Tamara said.

"No, you didn't let me. You girls are slow, and men are faster, isn't that so Dad?" he turned to me and asked.

"Of course men are faster," I said, giving in to him, because we all had to give in to him, since he was the youngest and favorite to all of us.

"Come on, now, sit down and have some breakfast. It is in the kitchen on the table. Your mother's made what you like and I want to see who will be the first to eat it and then go to school," I told them. While Isabela and I were drinking coffee and talking, the children were having breakfast. I was thinking how happy and carefree they were. They have changed a lot in the last ten years.

Tamara was only four and a half when we came to America, and she is already in the eleventh grade and attends Douglas Freeman, a very good school. She still has an innate blond lock of hair on her head, and she is a real beauty. Ogi was only ten months old when we came, and he now goes to the sixth grade. He loves wrestling and WWE, so when I return home from work he shows me how HHH, The Rock, Hulk Hogan fought. When I say I like Lita (a beautiful female wrestler) the best, he just turns around and says that I don't know anything. They love each other a lot and help each other when they need it. Naturally, Tamara helps Ogi more with school, but he gives her his sweets, and she does not mind it then.

My wife Izabela, although she is in her forties, is looking great. Nobody who sees her thinks that she is older than thirty. She still has a nice shape and beautiful features, and I am certainly proud of that. In the previous two years, she had been touched first by her mother's death, and then by our oldest daughter, Bojana's, marriage, and these two incidents both left a trace on her face, and probably in her heart too, but all in all she was fine. Even losses are part of life, and they must be accepted as such. Life does not stop; life moves on, and we must live for these two kids and guide them in the right direction.

After breakfast, the children got ready for school and we saw them off to the school bus. I finally went to the bathroom to have a shower and shave. While I was having a shower I heard knocking on the door.

"I'm going to work, I'm already late," my wife said. This was usual for her. "Think about what I've told you about visiting a psychologist. I'll call you," she added as she left.

"OK, I'll think about it," I replied lazily, although I believe she didn't hear what I said.

In time I realized I did, in fact, need to go, and so I resolved to make the appointment.

I dressed up nicely, as for a special occasion. Today was a big day for me: the day I would find out what was going on in my head. I felt sort of nervous, and before leaving I took a swig of whisky to relax. While I was driving towards the city I began to relax and enjoy the ride. I turned onto Parham Road, then onto 1-64 east towards the city. My Bonneville was sailing like a boat on water. On both sides of the road, there were colorful trees and some billboards. On one of those I saw that the lottery jack-pot was forty million. *Someone will become rich,* I thought. While passing the exit for Staples Mill, on which I turned off when I went to work, I saw on my left the familiar water tower on my company's grounds, with the inscription CADMUS. With the slow swinging of the car, I recalled how it had all begun.

At Cadmus

My relative Relja Milanović, who is now called Ray at work, applied for a job at Cadmus Printing Co. (a Cenveo Company) and he asked me, since he did not speak English at all, to accompany him on the interview and help him with translation. I spoke a little. I can can only imagine what kind of interview it is, when one of the men who is applying for the job does not speak the language at all, and his interpreter speaks very little. Nevertheless, he got the job in the department where the magazines are tied and packed, where he works even today, and I used that chance to apply for a job. I liked the company because it was very near, only seven or eight miles from my house, and so it took me only fifteen minutes to get to work, and it was a big company with great insurance. After a few days, to my surprise, they called me for an interview. I had the interview for the position of blue liner, and, of course, I had no idea what this job was about. When I arrived in front of the building, I was so nervous, as if I were about to talk with President Clinton. Everything I had learned to say at the interview the previous day, I naturally forgot when I looked across the table at the serious faces of Eddie Miller and Ville Wall. Most of my answers were "Yes" and "No," but I obviously pronounced them right and got the job.

Cadmus was originally founded in 1913 as William Byrd Press, employed over 500 workers and produced journals, magazines, catalogs, brochures, school textbooks and other print products. My job was in the pre-press department where I produced the final proof for customers before it was sent for printing. Using a blue light, we burned the images on special papers and made sure it was perfected before being sent out. I found that job very interesting, which made the hours pass quickly. At the beginning I was ashamed to start talking with the employees because of my lack of English knowledge, and I mostly talked with Ms. Eloise, a quiet, old worker who showed me what to do and how to do it. It wasn't a difficult job and everything began to get better. I met a lot of friends and I learned English more and more every day. After six months my strict manager in the pre-press department, Robert Maxwell, called Max, showed he was pleased with my work by moving me to the convention plate room. There, we exposed images from film onto plates, which then went to the printing press. I was on that post the following six months. After that, Max moved me to the post of a digital assistant, where we exposed the image on special plates by laser. Unfortunately, the very same computers that enhance production make people unnecessary, and because of all that computerization, a lot of workers were laid off. Among them were my good friends Wess, Bucky, Wally, Mark, Willie Wall, who employed me, and many others. Most of them had worked in the company for twenty to thirty years, but what can be done? That's capitalism and there's no mercy.

I spent most of my time with Mike, called Minnesota Mike because he moved from cold Minnesota to Virginia. His ex-wife got married to someone in Richmond and the kids were with her, so he moved to Richmond as well to be close to his children, leaving all his relatives and friends in Minnesota. He was the one who helped me most with my English, using a Webster dictionary that he had at work. He spelled each new word to me, looked it up in the dictionary and explained its meaning to me. Of course he taught me some words that are not for public writing, but that is also a part of life.

When we weren't at work, Mike and I spent a lot of time going to Renegades hockey matches, Braves baseball games and Kickers soccer matches. We became good friends and sometimes we would go with the others to Buffalo Wild Wings or Hooters, without the knowledge of our wives, of course.

Somehow, during one of my talks with Mike, I told him about the problems I was having. He listened to me attentively while I talked about the dreams that had been haunting me and about the part of my life that I didn't remember. When he had heard me out, to my surprise, he asked me why I didn't go to a psychologist. I told him that I was not crazy, at which he started laughing. I would never forget what he then said: "You Mickey," (that's what they call me at work) "still don't know where you live. America is a crazy country. Everybody has to have a lawyer, a doctor and a psychologist."

When he saw that I was looking at him, astonished, he continued, "You have to have a lawyer when you go to court. You have to have a doctor to take care of your health and to give you prescriptions for the pills you can't do without, and a psychologist to wash your brain and help you stay sane."

Today I can see that he was right and that everything he said was true. Three days after that conversation, to my surprise, he came to my house and told me to get dressed and come with him to the best psychologist he knew, because I had an appointment. At first I refused to go, but since he was persistent, I had to obey him in the end.

"Dr. Michael Smith" was written on the door of a big building on Monument Avenue. It was late fall and the leaves had fallen down onto the sidewalk and onto the grass in the park in front of the building. It was a beautiful part of town. The building was old, in the gothic style, with magnificent arches at the entrance and a statue of a lion on each side. We barely managed to open the heavy, carved oak door and entered the huge reception room. On both sides there were chairs, and in front of them, tables with a great number of magazines.

A young, charming girl was sitting at the reception desk. Her long, blonde hair was gently falling over her shoulders. A light shadow above her eyes revealed that she was a person who knew how to apply make up tastefully, and it gave to her beautiful blue eyes a kind of soothing deepness. She had sensual lips with dark red lipstick, and when she saw us she smiled, showing a perfect row of teeth, the whiteness and shine of which almost dazzled me.

"Hello, I'm Stacy. Can I help you?" she said in a resonant voice.

When he saw that I almost hadn't heard her question, being bewitched by her beauty, Mike at last said, "Hello, I'm Mike, and this is my friend Mickey. He has an appointment with Dr. Smith today."

"All right, sign your name in the register and give me your driver's license and insurance card to copy," Stacy said and smiled, distracting and confusing me even more.

When she had gone to the next room to make copies, Mike pushed me with his elbow in the ribs and said, "Wake up, you didn't come here to look at Stacy but to talk with Dr. Smith." And then he continued laughing.

Finally I wrote my name and surname, the time of the visit, the name of the insurance company and who knows what else in the register. Stacy returned and handed me my documents with a smile and said, "Thank you Mr. Milanović. The doctor will see you soon. Please take a seat and relax."

I sat down next to Mike and took a newspaper from the table, not even looking, and started leafing through it. I looked more above the newspaper at gorgeous Stacy than at the newspaper itself.

"I didn't know you read the newspaper upside down," Mike interrupted my thoughts. "You are really a case for a psychologist." And then he laughed. I looked at the newspaper and, curiously enough, I really was holding it upside down. When I turned it over, I looked at Stacy and noticed that she was smiling, probably because she'd heard what Mike had said. At that moment, on our right side, the door opened and Dr. Smith appeared. He was a tall man with a serious expression on his face and a refined haircut. Some grey hairs on his head disclosed he was a man of fifty-something. Behind the glasses, two black eyes were looking at me with a piercing stare. I had a feeling that he was reading what I was thinking.

At last, he said in a gentle voice that was not in accordance with his severe expression, "Milenko, you can come into my office." I was surprised that he called me by my real name, because many Americans find it too difficult to pronounce and use my nickname instead. I stood up, hypnotized, and as I passed by him I could smell a beautiful fragrance. I heard him say, "Mike, thank you for recommending me to Milenko. You can come later to pick him up or you can stay here and read something."

"All right, Dr. Smith, I have something to do so I will come back later," Mike said and left.

The door closed and Dr. Smith offered me a seat on a chair by his desk. His office wasn't big. Two walls were covered with shelves full of books, which were probably from his field of work. On the third wall, there was a big painting which I did not understand at all. It reminded me of when children put their fingers in paint and spread it around. Below the painting there was a chair and a kind of narrow bed. On the fourth wall was the door and next to it, a beautiful wood china closet, on which there were some flowers. Although the big lamp next to the door, as well as the one on his desk, were lit, I had the feeling that it was too dark in the room. I noticed that there were no windows at all in the office.

"Milenko," he said at last, "I am Dr. Michael Smith and I have been working as a psychologist for almost twenty-eight years. You may be surprised that I call you by your real name, but I can tell you that I've got several patients from your country and I have learned a lot of Serbian words with them. Mike is my friend, and he often talks about you and your problems. Although this is not a usual way of receiving a patient, since your GP should have sent you to me first, I made this exception because Mike insisted."

"Thank you doctor." My voice seemed more automatic than conscious. Dr. Smith talked in a gentle voice, as if he were singing, and that relaxed me. I was beginning to feel more and more at ease. We continued our conversation, which began to seem more like a conversation between two friends than between a doctor and patient. I told him my perspective on my life in Bosnia before and during the war, about my arrival in America and my life in Richmond. Naturally, I mostly talked about my bad dreams and the part of my life I was not able to remember. That part of my life was an illusion—a missing link. Dr. Smith listened to me attentively. During the conversation an hour flashed by like a minute.

After I had told him everything, Dr. Smith finally said, "I think that your trauma originates from something that we should find out in the following few months. You should be persistent and hold on till the end and with that the result will come. We will start the therapy next week and after that on a regular basis every two weeks. I will give you the final findings at the end when we finish with all the necessary therapy. We are through for today and we'll see each other next week. Stacy will make you an appointment."

He walked me to the door, said goodbye and told Stacy to put me on the schedule for the following week. When she had finished she gave me a card with information about my next appointment and she said with a kind smile, "We'll see you next week Mr. Milanović."

I saw Mike in the parking lot, nervously pacing like a pregnant woman before labor, waiting for me to arrive.

"Thank God you've finally finished. You are really a difficult case. Dr. Smith usually finishes with patients in twenty minutes the first time, and you've stayed for more than an hour," he started firing, sitting down in the car. On our way back we stopped at Buffalo Wild Wings and talked about all kinds of things. We didn't stay for a long time because he had to go to the other job he was doing for AAA insurance. In America, some people work two or three jobs, especially if they live by themselves and have big expenses.

The following months went by like a dream. Everything was as it had been before. Going to work, responsibilities at home, taking care of children, food shopping, dreams . . . The only change was my visits to Dr. Smith every other week. During each session I would lie on a leather sofa, and the doctor would sit on a chair near my head, and in a calming voice he would ask me completely ordinary things. I wasn't able to understand why the time went so fast, and I couldn't remember what we had talked about for so long. At the end of every conversation, Dr. Smith would smile mysteriously at me and encourage me to keep going the way I was. I didn't know what he meant by that, but it pleased me to see beautiful Stacy every time and talk with her a little. Although I didn't comprehend Dr. Smith's therapy, thinking that I was wasting my time going there, every time I left his office I felt a little bit more relaxed and calmed. My night dreams had in time lost their power and they happened less and less often. I didn't take any pills, but Dr. Smith would give me tea, which he called Russian tea, although I don't know why; it didn't look at all like the tea I had at home. The members of my family neither knew nor noticed that I had been seeing a psychologist, since I usually told my wife that I was going to work or food shopping, which I would finish after the therapy.

I turned onto Boulevard Avenue and then onto Monument Avenue. At last I saw the familiar building where Dr. Smith's office was. I parked in my usual spot behind the building and went inside. As always, charming Ms. Stacy was sitting at the reception desk with a beautiful smile, which was a real refreshment.

"How are you, Mr. Milanović?" she asked.

"Fine, thanks, and you Stacy?" I replied.

"Excellent, thank you," she said and added, "I hope this is not your last visit to our office and that you will stop by to see us sometime."

"Of course I will Stacy," I said, "I would like to see such a beautiful and charming girl every day."

"Thanks for the compliment," she replied with a mysterious smile and said, "Dr. Smith is expecting you. Go in."

I knocked on the door and when I opened it, I saw Dr. Smith sitting behind his desk, which was covered in papers. When he lifted his head, he smiled and showed me with his hand to the chair opposite him. I sat down.

"How do you feel today, Milenko?" he asked.

"Very well, doctor, and you?" I answered.

"I'm fine," he said and continued, "As you know, today is your last visit. I must admit, I am very glad I've met you. I've never had a case like yours before. It has been a great pleasure listening to you and hearing of your problems, which I believe will go away when you read this." At this, he pointed to the yellow envelope in front of him. "You will find here the lost part of your life that has been haunting you. Here you will read about the sad part of your past. Although it is sad, you should be proud, because it is a part of you and it will stay impressed in your soul as long as you're alive."

Then he continued explaining to me how and why the memory loss began, using medical terms, most of which I didn't understand. I impatiently waited to be given the envelope and to see what it contained.

After twenty minutes, he got up from the chair, and I knew he had finished and that it was time for me to say goodbye and leave his office. He handed me the envelope with a smile and told me to stop by to see him. As though hypnotized, I tightly clenched the envelope because I was afraid that it might fall out or run away somehow.

I remember offering him my hand and saying goodbye with a promise that I would stop by again. I waved to Stacy while passing by her, who saw me off with a smile. I sat down in the car and caught my breath, setting the mysterious envelope down on the seat beside me. I looked at it and had the feeling that it was looking at me, too. I took it and opened it slowly. To my surprise I saw a book. It was titled *Muslim's Camp at Visoko 1992-93*, by Milenko S. Milanović.

Different thoughts and questions without answers went through my head: *Where? Who? How? About what? Why?* Slowly, almost with fear, I turned to the first page and read, *The Diary, June 20, 1992.* I felt like something exploded in my head. I tasted the same dry earth in my mouth and sensed the very same explosion and darkness from my dreams . . .

I took a deep breath. It was like I had been struck by lightning. With shaking hands I quickly closed the book and threw it onto the seat next to me. My heart felt like it would jump out of my chest. I was breathing heavily, and only when I had taken a big sip of already cold coffee did I start to regain control of myself again. I calmed down a little and tried not to look at the book as I started the car and drove home. During the ride, I cast a glance at it a few times, and it stared back at me. Passing by a 7-11, I stopped and bought a newspaper.

When I arrived home, I first poured myself a big glass of whiskey and took a big swallow. I had the feeling that I was rinsing from my mouth the bitterness of the earth, which I could still taste. After the second glass of whiskey I gathered courage, took the book in my hands and decided to read it. It couldn't be that I'd gone to see Dr. Smith so many times for nothing. I sat down in a comfortable armchair, put the whiskey next to me, and opened the book. My eyes filled with tears. I started reading, squinting . . .

About two months after my emotions settled down, the dreams stopped and I had started to live a peaceful life, I visited Dr. Smith to talk to him about the book and how he came upon it. He told me that my unusual case had prompted him to do research on Yugoslavia's war. This led to his discovery that there was a book in Belgrade about a camp for Serbs in Visoko during the war.

Shortly after, one of his patients from Richmond, born in Serbia, visited Belgrade and brought him back the book—my book—the book I had suppressed my memories of. In it he discovered the cause of all of my nightmares.

An Aerial Photograph of the Visoko Prisoner of War Camp

A   Camp building
B   Bus station
C   Croats Monastery
D   Railroad Sarajevo Šamac
E   City Hall and court building

F   River Bosna
G   Serbs territory
H   Hotel Visoko
I   River Fojnica

THE DIARY

Slow Dying

Saturday, June 20, 1992

Light shaking of the lorry's tires on the macadam wakes me up. I am lying down. I open my eyes and see familiar faces. I have a terrible headache. I put my hand under my head for a moment and feel something sticky. My bloody hand brings me back to reality. In the lorry, together with me, are my relatives, friends, neighbours. I remember shooting, explosions, a rifle cocking behind my back and a bang on the head. They picked us all up from our homes and are driving us somewhere. But where are the women and children? There are only men here. Nobody knows and nobody says anything. When I lift my head I see familiar surroundings. They drive us through Poriječani to Visoko. While driving alongside the railway, we can see that the Serbian houses in the settlement of Pučište and Donja Zimća are on fire. The lorry is full, but nobody says a word. Everybody is frightened. We arrive in Visoko at the military barracks called Janko Balorda, where the Yugoslav army had been before the war began. The lorry stops, and the guards drive us out shouting, "Get out, you mother fucking Chetniks, faster . . . !"

They beat anyone they can with feet, hands, rifle butts. I rub my eyes, not knowing whether this is a dream or reality. They lock us up in the cellar of an old building without any light or windows. After two or three hours, they take us out into a corridor and write down our names, dates of birth, places of residence, professions.

I see here my former math professor, Zijad Kadrić, called Zijo. He smiles and nods his head. After that, they take us to the first floor of the building to Room 3. They close the door. There are some people here who were already locked in before us, and

21

among them are my father and my uncle. I am glad they are alive. I smile to my dad and nod my head to say that everything is okay. Nobody dares to speak aloud; we only whisper. I sit down in the corner with Boban, Vase, Vukan, Dragan and Dejan, who was wounded in both hands and bleeds. I tear up someone's undershirt and wrap his hands with it. He whispers to me that they killed my relative Vladimir Milanović and that Gojko Duvnjak has been wounded. We sit on the hard parquet. The night comes down, and the room gets fuller and fuller. Forty-three, sixty-eight, eighty-two, one-hundred and fifteen, one-hundred and forty . . . We don't even have enough room to sit. The room is full, and nobody says a word. Fear, uncertainty . . .

Sunday, June 21, 1992

My whole body hurts because of the parquet floor. I wasn't able to sleep. I was thinking about the previous day. Is it luck or not to be here? I am a bit consoled by the fact that the warden, Zijad Kadrić, is my old friend and a former teacher at the secondary school. He used to be a good man, but now . . . now I don't know. Dejan's hands bleed, and we don't have bandages. People sit on the floor like chickens, and they are silent. They are all terrified and think about what will come next. Why have they locked us here? Are we guilty for this damned war? I peep out through the window and see familiar faces, yesterday's friends, neighbors, acquaintances, colleagues, teammates from football . . . and in the room . . . in the room, a Serb next to a Serb. Three generations of the same family: grandfather, son, grandson, from the families of Milanović, Marković, Krsmanović . . .

Inside the room, fear and hunger. While whispering among ourselves, I find out that the family Vuković was executed by a firing squad on their doorstep. Families Ristić and Damjanović were shot in the same way. Yesterday Višnja Bajić was killed, and her father Boban was wounded while he was dragging her to hospital. She used to be a very pretty girl of only ten. In the same way Igor Stojčić, a son of Ivica, was killed. My relative Gordan Ćulum was wounded in his right leg. Dragan Cvijetić, called Branko, committed suicide because he didn't want to surrender to the Muslims. In just one day more than twenty people were killed. The watchman in the camp is Lopo Nezir.

We make a list of camp inmates by rooms. The commanders of the changing of the guards are well known to us: Burko Suljo, Burko Šačir, Besim Kulović and Sead Kadrić, called Šicko, who is a brother of the camp warden, Zijad. Last night the guards beat someone from Room 4 in the corridor, but we don't know who it was. We are hungry, but that is not important now.

June 22, 1992

It is too cramped to sleep, since we all have to be on our sides so we can all lie down. If you have to go to the toilet, when you come back you no longer have the place where you used to lie. We are like lined sardines. Room 3 is seventeen meters long, and seven meters wide, which is 117 square meters in total, and there are 154 camp inmates in the room. We don't even have one square meter at our disposal.

They took away my uncle Miloš from the room. Finally they brought sliced bread in a dirty army blanket and they shook it out onto the floor like we were animals. The people fight for a crust of bread because of the starvation. Many of them did not manage to grab their share. It is sad to see how people fight over a slice of bread like hungry dogs. They brought Uncle Miloš back into the room. He is blue all over from the beatings. The blood runs down his head. His hands and legs are blue from the blows. He shakes with fear. I put damp cloths on his body, since that's all we have. When I see him crying, I become more and more afraid. *Why?* I ask myself almost continuously why this is all happening, but there is no answer.

The people are nervous, hungry, afraid. Finally they bring us food in the evening and pour it into some old army dishes. Beans with meat. Great. We don't have spoons, so we eat with our fingers or by leaning the dish onto our mouths. We eat like pigs. Awful and sad, but it doesn't matter as long as we eat.

Tuesday, June 23, 1992

They beat Uncle Miloš again. When they went into his house to rob it, they found among his books his university student's booklet, where they saw that his professors at that time had been Biljana Plavšić and Dr. Nikola Koljević, who are now in the Serbian Democratic Party (SDS) and in the government of the Republic of Srpska. He was beaten by Namik Dizdar, Elmedin Ahmić and Hasan Čizmić. They accused him of being a sniper. How can he be a sniper and not be able to see the television from seven to eight meters away? Uncle Miloš did not serve in the army because he was shortsighted. These accusations cannot be the real reason they beat him. It seems they are just an excuse. They are former students of his, to whom he taught the Serbian language. He would not give passing grades to them until they learned the lessons, so they are now trying to get revenge on him by beating him. It is an excuse to humiliate their teacher so he can see who they are now. Uncle Miloš is a man of about fifty, a teacher of Serbian, Russian and French, and he was a very strict teacher. He has devoted all his life to books and learning, and he was not interested in anything else in life. He has never married. If he deserves to be beaten, I can only imagine what will happen to the others.

I found out that the women from the vicinity of Visoko are locked in the Room 1, and the men in the Rooms 2, 3 and 4. I suppose there are over 400 of us in the camp.

Wednesday, June 24, 1992

They beat Saša Krsmanović last night, and his father and grandfather cry, but they cannot help him. Everything hurts Uncle Miloš. On his back are the marks from the pickax handle. A scab formed on his head and it is no longer bleeding. He is afraid they will beat him again. I try to convince him that they won't, but I don't believe it myself. They have beaten some men from the other rooms, but we don't know who. We can only feel the walls and floors shaking when they beat someone. In a silent night, screams, moans and the crying of the camp inmates echo. We can't sleep because our hips and shoulders hurt from the hard oak floor on which we lie, and because we are afraid and wait for them to take one of us to beat. It is sad how yesterday's friends, if they really were friends, have changed and become criminals overnight. I can't comprehend what it is in human beings that makes a beast out of a man.

Thursday, June 25, 1992

"Misfortunes don't come singly"—that is the case with Uncle. He had to write a statement and was beaten for the third time. He wrote that a state cannot be made like the backward Muslim peasants are trying to do, and that Alija Izetbegović did not conceive democracy like this, but it only harmed him. He confessed his sins to me, because he didn't think that he would survive. We cried together. I tried to comfort him by saying that he would stay alive, but even I did not believe that.

Friday, June 26, 1992

There is a chaos in the room. It is hot, cramped, and that damned parquet does not allow us to get any sleep. If only we had a blanket to put under us. A pillow would be a sheer luxury. Our beards have already grown long and we are dirty from sweat. I have almost forgotten the feel of a toothbrush and toothpaste.

They give us food three times a day and it is tasty. On purpose or by chance, they salt it excessively and then they don't give us any water. It is hot outside. We die of thirst. The little water we have, we save, so we can apply damp cloths to our skin after the beatings. We also moisten our lips with damp cloth, since we don't have enough to drink. We have to save each drop. Through the window we can see the Muslims washing their cars and trucks with water running unnecessarily, and they still don't give us a proper drink.

My uncle has a fever and talks nonsense. I asked the warden to bring a doctor to check Dejan's arms, which have begun to smell bad. The doctor came in the afternoon and I took Dejan to the warden's office. When the doctor unwrapped his arms, which I had wrapped with unclean shirts, since it was the only thing we had, I smelled the worst stench in my life. Some kind of yellow fluid was running down from the wounds on his forearms. His wounds had become infected, and the flesh around them had begun to decay. The doctor said that he would have to take him to the health centre in Visoko, where they would clean and sew up the wounds.

Dejan and the other wounded man, Gojko, were taken to the health centre in Visoko, and when they returned after two hours, their arms were wrapped with clean bandages, but they had bruises on their bodies and faces. The doctor told Dejan that he should go every day to have his bandages changed, but he is afraid of beatings and will not go again.

Saturday, June 27, 1992

They gave us water after two days, but now they don't allow us to go to the toilet. When they do let someone go out to the corridor or the toilet, they beat him up, so we don't feel like leaving the room, but we must. We can choose either to piss in our pants or to get beaten. One doesn't know which is worse.

In the room there are young men and old men, healthy and ill, insane and sane, but I can still see pride in their eyes in spite of everything we are going through now. The people encourage one another and they pray to God to help us to not become discouraged. We will endure. The Serbs have always been brave and persevering. We endured five hundred years under the Ottoman Empire in the Balkans, so we can probably endure a few months or years in the camp of Visoko. If only they would let the old people and the ill go home. In Room 3 are the sick people: Slavko Koprivica, who is diabetic; Branivoj Radulović, called Zane, who suffers from tuberculosis; Milan Kačar, who is schizophrenic; Slavko Topalović, who suffers from cancer; and others.

From the list of the camp inmates we can see that there are whole families in the camp. The greatest in number is my family; there are twenty-two Milanovićs, then eighteen Vanovacs, eleven Cvijetićs, nine Krsmanovićs . . .

Sunday, June 28, 1991 – St. Vitus's Day

A great Serbian Saint. Today an executioner from Visoko, Hajrudin Halilović, called Mrčo, came into the room. He is a brother of the commanding officer of the Muslim army for Bosnia and Herzegovina, Sefer Halilović. They were born and grew up in the village Orahovo, near Kozarska Dubica. Mrčo wants arms from us, and claims that all Serbs have three rifles each, alluding to the fact that we cross ourselves with three fingers: in the name of the Father, Son and the Holy Ghost. We don't even know who this man is, or how much sorrow and trouble he will bring us in the months ahead.

Like on every other Serbian holiday, today the Muslims attack Čekrčići. They are trying to build a road to connect Zenica with Sarajevo by cutting through the Serbian municipalities of Ilijaš, Semizovac, Vogošća, Ilidža and others. The first line of the separation between the Serbs and the Muslims is about five hundred meters away from the center of Visoko, whereas the buildings that were turned into a camp for the Serbs are about three hundred meters away by air. We are separated from the Serbian territory by the river Bosnia.

The Muslims shell the Serbian positions from the barracks camp every day, two to three hours before the infantry attack on the Serbs, and then they turn on the sirens for the air attack and lie to the Muslim citizens of Visoko, saying that the Serbs have attacked Visoko. The cannons that they use to fire at the Serbian positions are under the window of our room, and we watch as the shells hit the Serbian positions.

The Muslims know that the Serbs won't shoot at the army barracks, since we are locked in the camp and represent a live shield for the Muslims. We hear detonations and the fighting from the theater of operations every day, and we pray to God that the Serbs can endure the attacks.

Tuesday, June 30, 1992

Hot and stuffy. Nura comes to the room. Lazo Vanovac, called Car, Dragomir Vanovac, called Cundo, Nešo Vanovac, Mladen Raković and Branivoj Radulović beaten up.

[Nura was a hairdresser who had lived in Ilijaš and then fled to Visoko and there harassed women in the camp of Visoko—she entered the room and greeted us with "Akšam hajrula." In fear, some answered with "Allah rasola" (a response to the Muslim greeting), and then she cursed our "Chetnik mothers" and started beating everyone around her with a nightstick.]

Wednesday, July 1, 1992

Bager interrogated again—crying because of alleged threats to his wife and children. Says he got several slaps in the face. I am suspicious of that.

[Bager was interrogated the longest and most often and left the camp on July 7, 1992, under dubious circumstances.]

Thursday, July 2, 1992

Suddenly some soldiers with untidy hair and beards enter the room and start beating one person after another. One of them is wounded in the arm. They speak some foreign language. The camp inmates are driven to the corners of the room like sardines, and one of the soldiers, with a knife in his hand, goes around the room and chooses the inmates he is going to beat. Fear and silence have taken over. One can hear a fly flying. They take my relative Željo and start beating him in front of us. After that they beat Vukan on the head with batons. After that, Zoran Topalović, who faints . . .

All of a sudden the warden enters the room and drives the soldiers out. From the corridor, we can hear the uproar as the warden reprimands Šačir for allowing the soldiers to come into the room. It seems they have been beating in other rooms as well. We stand against the wall. After half an hour, the warden comes back into the room, and when he sees us so terrified, he tells us to sit down and that those soldiers, who were from the front, will not come again. Should we trust him?

ROOM NUMBER 3

A hundred and fifty-seven in one room
We were cramped as such,
But when tormentors came inside
It could have fit twice as much.

They start beating everyone

And a brother hides behind a brother,
And people run like beasts
To stay alive they would rather.

To run away from hell there is no way
As we cannot break the wall,
To pray to God is only what's left
To stop the tormentors from beating us all.

And they beat, and keep on beating
Just like children the people moan
As beatings are hard for everyone
Some cry, and some weep alone.

When everything is finished, and they leave,
Against the wall we silently stand, a lot,
We sadly look at each other
But to move . . . no, we dare not.

Friday, July 3, 1992

"It has started, it sure has."—Napoleon before the battle at Waterloo.

They call out eight people from our room. From other rooms, the same. The camp inmates line up in a file and exit the building into the yard. We watch through the window. They take up tools and dig trenches in the barracks, because, allegedly, the Muslims expect an attack from the Serbian side. A lie. The camp inmates dig the trenches, and the criminals walk from one to the other, hitting them with rifle butts, feet, batons, pickax handles. In the shade, under a tree, Mrčo sits and his tormentors bring him camp inmates one by one from the canal. Each camp inmate has to squat, crouch or bend on his knees and elbows, and then they beat him. Mrčo and his tormentors—Miralem Čengić, Amir Murtić, Esnaf Pulić, called Esno, and Samir Selimović, called Domac—vent their anger on the innocent civilians, honest citizens. I recall when I worked in the Magistrate Court in Visoko, I sent Domac to prison because of various offenses. He got this nickname because he grew up in penitentiaries. Domac is a short form of the word 'penitentiary' in Serbian—or whichever language you're referring to. Now he has the law in his hands—the law of the wooden handles and electric cables he beats us with. I am afraid even to even think about what will happen to me when I go out to dig, since it is certain that my turn will also come.

I can see my relatives Boban, Vaso, Djordje, Jovan, Mladen, my friends Guge, Šoja, Ratko and the others in the canal. They took from my relative Djordje a golden watch and six hundred German marks, and they paid him in beatings. Awful.

Saturday, July 4, 1992

Again, the digging of the canal and beatings. Everything is the same; just the people are different. This time they took Zdravko and Jovo Milanović, Zoran Čivčić, Jovo Ljepić and Stojko Krsmanović from our room and many others from other rooms. Mrčo came to our room and ordered us to make a list of weapons that we had left at home or he would start killing us. I wrote the list of weapons, which a few of us had legally. We didn't know if the weapons were still in our houses, though, or if someone had taken them already. We have been imprisoned for fifteen days now and don't know what is going on in our houses. I went with Mrčo and Halim Zukić, who was the driver, and whom I personally knew since we used to work in the same building. From Room 2, Radovan Živanović came with us, and from Room 4, Slobodan Tokić. When we arrived in our settlement, I almost didn't recognize the place where I used to live. Everything was plundered, knocked down; doors and windows were taken from the houses, cars were stolen, domestic animals were taken. Only the pigs had been killed, since the Muslims' religion forbids them from eating pork.

At my house, the garage door was open, and my car, an Opel Cadet, was taken. I saw my mother and other women in Kalotići. Not a man in sight since all of them were in the camp. Even women were imprisoned in the centers in Hlapčevići and Buzić Mahala, and they were not allowed to go home until their neighbours had finished stealing everything they wanted from the Serbian houses.

The guns we were looking for were found and handed over to Mrčo. On the way back, I said hello to my mother, who was in tears and asked Mrčo if we could take some food to the camp inmates. He allowed that. On the ride back, Mrčo asked me for five hundred German marks to let me go from the camp, but I didn't have that kind of money, so now I remain in the camp to experience everything that follows.

July 5, 1992
They took out five of us from our room to mow the grass on the camp grounds. In my group, together with me were Stamenko, called Stame, Vaso, Rajko and Dragan. We worked and nobody touched us. After we had finished, we even washed our faces and socks on the hydrant. It was a real refreshment. On our way back to the room, the guard let us pick the plums and take them to the room. Finally, one peaceful day.

Monday, July 6, 1992
Mowing of grass and the first beating—Vase, Stame, Rajko Aksić, Dragan Živanović and I. Domac and Esno the waiter beat us on our backs with an iron bar. Rajko fainted, and I carried him to the room. Stame says that they beat me most, about some thirty blows on the back, which I did not even feel in my fear, except for the constant pain now. They asked about my wife—where she was, where she used to work, why wasn't she in the Territorial Defense (TO). Pain, and there is no lunch. In the afternoon they take me for interrogation to the investigating judge from Višegrad. He tells me that he knows all about the stations and that I should not try to lie to him. He shows me the report made by Branko "Bager" Raković.

[My wife Izabela worked in the laboratory of the former JNA in Visoko, and later in the military hospital in Sarajevo. She took refuge in Pale with the children before the war. They inquired why she had not gone to work for their Muslim army in the hospital in Visoko.]
[During interrogation, it was customary to beat up the man first and then to ask him about personal data.

There were rumours that the investigator was from Višegrad, a city in eastern Bosnia]

[The investigator told me about the statement of Branko Raković, in which he confessed that I had procured the radio station.]

Tuesday, July 7, 1992

Beating at the canal again. They beat us with handles, sticks, clubs and their feet. They are taking away everything from money to rings and watches. In the afternoon, Vase, Mirko Jošić, Bager, the Aksić family and Zdravko Ciganović were taken away from the room. Lucky them.

[This is when the first prisoner exchange took place]

Wednesday, July 8, 1992

Canal digging and beatings again. They make Vukan shout "Allahu akbar" at the top of his voice in the yard. Later, in the room, Boban advises him how to speak through his nose. There is humour even in fear. A new development—they no longer give us breakfast and supper. We do not know why.

[After the first exchange, when fifteen men were released, we were denied breakfast and supper and left with only lunch.]

Thursday, July 9, 1992

Canal digging and in the afternoon, Father and Uncle go home—exchanged. Fine, it has started.

[In the second exchange, when seventy-four men were released, my father and uncle were also exchanged.]

Friday, July 10, 1992

Another attack. Grenades. Canal digging, beatings. Nenad Vanovac below us. Boban at the canal.

[Nenad Vanovac (son of Jovo) was the organizer of

our defense and because of that he got beaten up the most. He was taken into the premises below ours almost every day and beaten there, knocked unconscious and carried back to the room, but he heroically endured it all.]

Sunday, July 12, 1992 – St. Peter's Day

Another Serbian Saint, another attack by the Muslims on the Serbian positions. It thunders the whole day. During the night, we watch the path of the tracer bullets, which travel as a swarm of bees. During the day, the siren for the air attack and the cannons that fire under our window. From the Serbian side, they answer back to the shelling and the shells fall inside the camp. The Muslims run hysterically, and we, being extremely happy, observe all this by peeping through the window. The shells fall closer and closer. We lie down on the floor. Shell fragments fly into the room and hit the ceiling, and the plaster comes off. The room is full of dust.

Finally, a day without beatings. We are getting thinner and thinner.

July 13, 14, 15, and 16, 1992

Every day the same. Digging of trenches and canals, beatings, sirens for danger, cannon fire under the window, grenades, only one meal a day. People fainting. Hot, and there is no water. Fear and beating up by Mrčo's gang. Nenad V., Saša K.

Friday, July 17, 1992

Canal digging. A grenade fell and wounded nine inmates—Saša M., Njonja, Djidja, Duci, Željko S., Milenko Despotović, Davor Glišić, Radulović, and Stojko Krsmanović. Saša, Njonja, and Radulović were severely injured and transferred to Zenica. After they had received medical assistance—and beatings—in the Health Center Visoko, the other slightly wounded camp inmates were put into the attic of the camp building where a dispensary had been made out of one room. They were taken to the health centre in Visoko. Muste Dedić.

[A shell that fell in the yard of the military barracks when trenches were being dug wounded Saša Milanović (son of Zdravko), Sladjan Šljivić (son of Risto), Jovo "Djidja" Krsmanović (son of Ostoja), Duško "Duci" Raković (son of Jovo), Željko Šljivić (son of Simo), Milenko Despotović, Davor Glišić (son of Ratko), Stojko Krsmanović, Branivoj "Zane" Radulović.]

[Health centre—they were first beaten up there and then treated for wounds.]

[Mustafa Dedić, nicknamed "Muste," the ambulance driver in the outpatient clinic in Visoko, beat up everybody who came to the health centre to ask for help. That is how he later killed Vojno Raković.]

Sunday, July 19, 1992

At last someone goes home—only old men: Dobro Glišić, Ostoja Krsmanović, Djordjo Glišić, Nedjo Cvijetić, Ostoja Milanović, Sreto Krsmanović, and others.

[Sreto Krsmanović died at home three days after he was released from the camp]

July 20, 21, 22, 1992

They interrogate us now about a Serbian army formation in Visoko that does not exist, and they want the arms from us that we do not have. We don't dig the canals because of the danger from shells. We have a bit more time, so I can write down everything about the past few days in my diary. Hunger takes its toll. People faint. I watch a fly walking on the face of a camp inmate, and he hasn't got the strength to drive it away. Our lips are chapped like oak bark. Many haven't been to the toilet for a month. It's hard to believe.

Thursday, July 23, 1992

We learned that Sreto Krsmanović died at home. He just managed to die at home like a man. A shame. The agony continues. Djordjo Bajić got a whole package of sugar cubes and each of us got two cubes so as to distribute it evenly. A real treat.

Thanks to him. If he had left everything for himself, he could have had it for two months. A generous gesture.

Friday, July 24, 1992
New releases. Joja, Žika Glišić and Radulović.

Saturday, July 25, 1992
First bathing after thirty-six days, without soap, towels or clean underwear.

> [We were allowed to take a bath for the first time after thirty-six days spent in the camp, in summer weather, in the heat, after labouring, beatings, digging the soil, sleeping on the floor.]

Wednesday, July 29, 1992
I saw Saka in the toilet yesterday. He is now in Room 4. He told me how he found out that his son had been killed. He said that a few days ago, a killer named Nisat Ramić had come into their room and beaten the inmates, one by one. Then he came to Saka, and when he recognized him, he couldn't hit him. As Ramić turned around and went out of the room, Saka recognized around his neck his son's golden cross necklace, which he had bought him. He knew then that his son was dead, since he had never taken that necklace off, nor would he let anyone take it off of him as long as he was alive. Unfortunately, that was exactly how it happened. Saka guessed it was a guilty conscience that kept Ramić from hitting him. He probably thought it was punishment enough that he had already killed his wife and son. That was a sad but true way to find out that your son was killed by someone who used to be a friend and who was very often a guest at your house.

Sunday, August 2, 1992
Fifty of us are transferred to Room 5 because of the alleged exchange. Immeasurable joy, but also uncertainty. "Z" came and brought food, Goran Šćepanović was also there.

[For reasons of security, the name of a Muslim, who is my friend, has been omitted. In the further text the sign "Z" will always have the same meaning]

[Goran Šćepanović was a Serb in the military police of the Muslim army—my former colleague from work.]

Monday, August 3, 1992

No exchange for the time being. I worked in the yard. Later, they called Vukan and beat him with a club, handles and sticks. He is ill and sweating all over. White as a sheet. We put poultices on him. Radenko V., Zoran C. and Jovo Blagojević in prison.

[As the interrogations drew to an end, we were gradually taken down to the cellar where the prison was, and every thirty days men were taken from this prison to the prison in Zenica and also to trial.]

Tuesday, August 4, 1992

They took some of the camp inmates after the investigation to the Municipal Court Visoko to a trial for taking part in the enemy Serbian army, and after that they locked them up in a regular prison which was separated from the camp. They were convicted of something for which they hadn't been guilty; they had been at their homes the whole time. It looks like even those houses were the enemy houses to the Muslims and that's the reason why they rob them now and take everything they want from them.

The Muslims were acting out a legal state, so they had appointed a Croat, Srećko Kitić, as municipality procecutor, and the judge was Mirko Lečić, a Serb converted to Islam, both of whom weren't allowed to make decisions alone; they had to do as they were told. We all wanted to be sentenced, since the convicts had much better treatment than camp inmates. They were imprisoned in a regular prison where they had beds, clean underwear and bed linen, regular meals, baths, shaving and, above all, nobody was allowed to beat them. After a verdict had been given, those prisoners were transferred to the prison in Zenica, which was a real professional prison for law breakers even during the time of Yugoslavia, and it was a real paradise compared with the camp in Visoko.

During the time of Yugoslavia and President Tito in this very same prison in Zenica, the present leader of the Muslims, Alija Izetbegović, was imprisoned because in his book, *The Islam Declaration,* he had expressed Muslim nationalism and stirred the Muslims up against the Christians.

Wednesday, August 5, 1992

Officially confirmed that there will be no exchange. Things go on as usual. We are in constant fear of who will go to prison in Zenica. Mrčo roll-called ten of us to go to Kozarci to look for weapons in the houses of Pipo Savić and Drage Kapur. We searched everything, but found nothing. We ate our fill of apples. I brought another bag of onions to the room. Everyone grabbed them—a real treat.

[Kozarci—a place near Visoko in the local community of Gornja Zimća—which is in the vicinity of our houses. Serbs from Zimća managed to get through towards the Croat village of Kiseljak and get out alive. From there they were transported to Ilijaš. The Muslim authorities suspected that there were still some arms in Kozarci, so they took us there to look for them]

[Jefto Savić, nicknamed Pipo, was one of the organizers of the defense and breakthrough towards Kiseljak]

Thursday, August 6, 1992

A sudden visit from the International Red Cross from Geneva. They registered all of us and they asked us about the living conditions in the camp. We complained of hunger and beatings. After they left, the guards started beating us because we had complained. Trifko "Trivo" Glišić, Milo Krunić, Živko Skopljak, Jovo Radosavljević and some others were beaten badly because of the complaints. They were beaten by the guards Dizdar, Čizmić, Ahmić, Genjac and Fejzić. During the torturing of the camp inmates, various tormentors cheer each other on. It happens often that one camp inmate is forced to drag another who is sitting on an army blanket. The one who is sitting has to beat with a cane or whip the inmate who is dragging him with shouts of "gee Chetnik," like when you drive a horse pulling a carriage. If the guards, who watch from both sides of the corridor, don't like the intensity of the blows, then they will beat the one who is sitting.

They usually use wooden batons, electric cables, mallets, whips, nightsticks, metal rods, rifle butts, feet, hands . . . The beatings most often happen in the shift of commanders Suljo Burko and Šacir Burko.

Friday, August 7, 1992

A new punishment came because we complained to the Red Cross. Next to the entrance of the room they put a plastic can of about twenty litres. We didn't know what we should use it for, but we soon found out. When one camp inmate knocked on the door and asked to go to the toilet, the guard told us that we weren't allowed to knock on the door anymore or we would be beaten, and from now on, we pissed and defecated in the can until the Red Cross came again. We couldn't believe what we heard. This was our future toilet. In the beginning it was strange, but when you have to, you get used to it. While you piss, only a meter away a hundred people watch you. With the number of camp inmates in the room, the can was filling up very quickly and it often overflowed onto the parquet.

Sunday, August 9, 1992 – St. Pantheleon's Day

A new attack on Ilijaš on every Serbian Saint's Day as a rule. Shooting all day. Grenades falling around us again and everything is shaking.

August 11, 1992

The visit of the Red Cross from Geneva again. We finally got soap for a bath and for washing clothes. It smells so nice. Since we are hungry, and the camp administration cannot feed us sufficiently, or it doesn't want to, we asked the Red Cross to allow our parents or our family to visit and bring food from home. The food in the camp is the same every day. Beans or rice with leeks, and sometimes, when we dig trenches, we get fish tins. We didn't dare complain to the Red Cross about the beatings. We had learned our lesson the last time. We asked them to bring us some blankets since we had been sleeping for almost two months on the hard wood parquet.

Wednesday, August 12, 1992

I don't know why, but we have been assigned to different rooms again. Just when you get used to someone and make friends, they then separate you. Again a bath. We now have soap. I am astonished to see how much weight people have lost over almost two months' time. They look like human skeletons on which a skin has been stretched, as do I probably.

Before the war, I used to watch films about the camps from the Second World War and I saw people so thin. I thought that it was impossible and that it was some kind of film editing. However, now that I see how thin the people here are, I realize it was authentic indeed. The people who used to weigh 120 kilos now weigh sixty. Our ribs look like piano keys on which you could play. My relative Rajko Milanović, who is a kind of entertainer in the camp, said on one occasion that if he sneezed, half of them would fall down onto the floor. The people are exhausted and hungry. Slow dying has been continuing in the camp Visoko.

Friday, August 14, 1992

At last, something cheerful. The visits of our parents have been approved. It looks like we will survive in some way. My mom will come today to see me after more than a month.

They called me out to the corridor because I had a visit. My mother. They had put tables in the middle of Room 6, which was empty, and in that way separated it into two parts, so we wouldn't have any contact with those who came to visit us. On one side there were parents, wives and families, and on the other side we—the camp inmates. Between us the tables, and on the tables . . . piles of food, the best in the world. When my mother saw me, she started crying and saying through tears, "How are you, son, why are you so skinny?" I couldn't say anything because of tears. I just shrugged my shoulders.

And what could I tell her and how could I explain to her that I was "full of everything," even life itself? And then my glance fell on all that food in front of me. *Dear God, thank you for letting me live to see all this wealth.* I started eating like a madman and cramming into my mouth everything that came to my hands: meat, pie, cheese, cream, cookies, coffee . . . There was only one thought in my head. I had to hurry, since we only had five minutes for the visit, and what you ate in that time was everything, and who knew whether you would ever eat again?

And my mouth . . . it felt like it had shrunk and was so small that it could not fit everything that I wanted to push inside. Why was it so small? And then the guard grabbed my arm and pushed me out to the room where I had been locked, since my five minutes had run out. I was still chewing food and when I had swallowed it, I remembered . . . my mother . . . she remained there crying, and I didn't even kiss her or say goodbye. She was left crying after her skinny and starved son. *Dear God, why are you doing all this to me . . . ?*

I came to the room, went inside, and a hundred hungry eyes were staring at me. They were silently asking whether there was something for them. They envied me because I had just eaten, and they were all hungry. I felt like killing myself.

Saturday, August 15, 1992

"Z" came to see me again. We talked about everything. I asked him to help Mother and Father. A bullet hit the wall above my head and threw cement on my head and in my eyes.

[Since our windows looked on Ilijaš, the Muslims shot through them, accusing those from Ilijaš for the firing.]

Thursday, August 20, 1992

Tina visits Luka and Jovan. I sent a message home in Djidja's boot.

[Kristina Milanović, nicknamed Tina, was wife of Luka and mother of Jovan]

Friday, August 21, 1992

Five Milanovićs—Luka, Zdravko, Jovan, Siniša and I—had to go and clean the riverbed of the river Bosnia. The sewage system from the camp, which went into the Bosnia riverbed, was blocked, and the whole town smelled. We dammed the river with rocks, changing its course, which cleaned the stagnant sewage system. Now the bigger part of the river flows by the army barracks. The guard who watched us, called Rus (a Russian), gave us a full bag of food which had been sent to Vukan. Since Vukan had already left for Zenica, Rus told us to eat it or he would throw it away. Naturally we ate it like hungry wolves, and thanked God that Vukan was in prison. Not even the smell in which we worked bothered us while we ate the delicious food.

Saturday, August 22, 1992

Brane Kokoruš was "interrogated" by Mrčo. Black and blue all over. Blood from his nose and eyes. Sirens sound air attack and then grenades on our positions and Ilijaš from the barracks. Our side returns fire at 8:30. This goes on all day. A sniper shot through the window and a bullet hit the wall half a meter above my head. It pierced my jacket and ricocheted against the wall into Drago Vanovac's back—there is no wound, only a bruise.

Sunday, August 23, 1992

Visoko was shelled again and the whole town was roaring. The Serbs will level it to the ground, God help them. In the evening we observe tracer bullets and shells coming from our positions to the Muslims. Our hearts are full of joy.

Monday, August 24, 1992

Finally calm—only individual sniper shots. Siniša, Djoka and Novica Milanović transferred from the camp to prison.

Tuesday, August 25, 1992

Mother-in-law and Vesna visit me at the gate and tell me

that many things in the town have been demolished. A grenade hit the roof of my brother-in-law's house. Tina sent a parcel. Jovan and Mladen Milanović, Djordjo Bajić, Uroš Vanovac, Zoran Damjanović, Milovan Raković transferred to prison from the camp. Tobacco arrived from Aco for Jovan and I must take it to him somehow in prison.

Wednesday, August 26, 1992

Dule Raković and Davor Glišić transferred from the dispensary to their rooms, still wounded and with shrapnel in their bodies. Three deserters put in our room. One of them provokes us and curses our "Chetnik mothers."

[In the attic of the house in which we were captives was a dispensary for those wounded during shelling while digging trenches.]

[Deserters of the Muslim army spent one to seven days in prison, and of their own free will returned to the front. They frequently deserted. Their heads were shaved upon their arrival at prison.]

Thursday, August 27, 1992

With my family in my thoughts—today is my daughter Bojana's birthday. She is eight. How are they celebrating it and are they thinking of me? Tankosa visits. The Mrdić family and Ljubomir Tešanović brought from Olovo.

[Lazo Mrdić, Mladjo Mrdić, Radomir Mrdić, Savo Mrdić, Sreto Mrdić. Arrested in Ilijaš at a place called Rakova Nova, all of them as civilians. In the camp they were said to be Chetniks. They were tortured so much that it was hard to recognize a human face.]

Friday, August 28, 1992

At last a bath for ten whole minutes, forty-eight of us under ten showers. Visit from the International Red Cross. I sent a message to Berlin and congratulated my daughters on their birthdays. Rajcin was beaten in the corridor—his leg.

[I sent the message through the Red Cross from Geneva.]

Saturday, August 29, 1992

A fateful day. Dizdar takes us down the stairs to Hamzić's office. It looks like the beatings are about to begin. I come inside where Mrčo and Hamzić are. They don't speak, just smile. Hamzić takes up a pickax handle. *Can it be that he is going to beat me with that?* They order me to stand with my shoulders against the wall. He draws back and hits me. I feel a terrible pain in my back. And then he alternately hits me with a fist in my jaws, then with the pickax handle on my back. *Oh, my God, will he ever stop?* I mechanically put my hand behind me to my save my back, and I feel my hand break with a blow. After I fall down, he kicks me in the jaw and the blood spatters on my T-shirt. After that, he stops. Dizdar takes me to the bathroom to wash my face and then to the room. The warden later finds out about the beating and asks me what happened. I tell him everything. Luka and Zdravko put a compress on me. Everything hurts.

OH, MY GOD!

Oh, my God,
Why do you torture us?
Why did we fall?
Why in the Islamic hands?
Damn the Turks all.

Oh, my God,
Where are you, if you exist?
Help the Serbian nation
And save us from these dogs
Show us the way to salvation.

Oh, my God,
Stop our torments,
Break our chains, then

Give us free hands
Since once we were called men.

Sunday, August 30, 1992

Drizdar calls me out again at 10:15 and we go down the stairs again. Again to Hamzić. He takes me out to the corridor where there are eight Muslim soldiers. He shows them my back and rear, which are blue, to demonstrate how to beat someone. I get dressed, and Mrčo stands with one foot on my toes, and with the other he kicks me in my genitals. After that they all press around me. They beat me with whatever they can—feet, hands, belts, and one who was wounded, with a crutch. At one moment, Esnaf Pulić, called Esno, grabs me around my waist, lifts me, and throws me onto the concrete. I hit my head and after that I can't remember anything. I was beaten by Esno, Murtić, Amir, Cikota, Domac, Miralem Čengić and a few others. When I regained consciousness I saw Nedžad Graho, who was carrying me to the room. They take me in and I lie on the floor. Luka and Zdravko again put damp cloths on my body. For a moment I lose consciousness again. Everything hurts me, and my left arm, which has started swelling, most of all.

Wednesday, August 31, 1992

In the morning the warden, together with Vojno Raković and Rade Terzić, takes me to health centre in Visoko to have my arm put in a cast. Again fear because you get the most beatings there. They x-ray my arm and put it in a cast. The whole time the warden is there with me and nobody touches me—they only curse. We finally get to the car where I see that Vojno is bleeding from the ear. I ask him "What's that?" and he only shrugs his shoulders. When we came to the camp, I carry him, with my arm in a cast, up the stairs to the room. Afterwards Rade, who was with him, told me that at the Health Centre Visoko he had been beaten by Mustafa Dedić, called Muste, who worked as a driver in the emergency squad. He hit him in the head with a knife handle. In the afternoon Vojno was moved to the attic, where the dispensary was, and his brother Boško was there, who looked after him and took care of him.

Wednesday, September 2, 1992

We find out that Vojno Raković died as a result of the beatings in the Health Centre. Muste Dedić killed him. We are all depressed and we are all sorry for Vojno, who was a very honest and peaceful man.

Sunday, September 6, 1992

At last a peaceful day without beatings. We are hungry. Three of us go out to clean the garbage around the containers. We go to the back part of the building with shovels and come to the garbage. The "garbage" is what remains of the food our families brought us two days ago, which we didn't have time to eat. All that nice and tasteful food is scattered around the containers and we . . . we are hungry. *Oh dear God in the sky if you exist, can you see this injustice?* Roasted pork, pie, bread, lard and everything else that the guards didn't like had been thrown away. We pick up the food and throw it into the container, and we cannot think about trying to take a bite. We don't dare, because behind us are executioners who are ready to satisfy our hunger in another way, very well known to them: with beatings.

Our visitors leave food with the guards, thinking that they will later give it to us to eat, and they don't know that after they go away the guards will take what they like for themselves and the rest they will throw away. And so we throw the food into the containers, and it smells so nice, but the smell doesn't come all the way to the stomach, just to the nose. We work hungry and cry, because that's the only way we can express our protest. *Oh, dear God, why are you doing this to us?*

Monday, September 7, 1992

Interrogations—Stamenko Krsmanović and Radovan Milanović. "Z" came again.

Tuesday, September 8, 1992

Nothing special happened. A member of Hrvatsko vijeće obrane—HVO (Croatian Defence Council) from Seoce, the hamlet of Kakanj, named Jure—was detained. He allegedly tried to transfer Serbs from Grančanica towards Vareš and Ilijaš. Two old people, seventy to eighty years of age, were arrested. The old man was beaten and the woman is caring for him in the attic.

Wednesday, September 9, 1992

The old man from Grančanica died as a result of the beating, while the old woman was "generously" allowed to bury him.

[Their names were Nikola and Mara Paradžina]

Thursday, September 10, 1992

Visiting day. Tankosa came and brought us food.

Friday, September 11, 1992

A bath. For lunch only a can of beef whose expiration date ran out a long time ago. We were supposed to have a visit, but it was postponed due to the war actions. The Muslims, as usual, fired at the Serbian positions from the cannons under our window. Then the Serbs answered the provocation. Three shells fell within the front of the camp. One hit a cannon and destroyed it and killed the Mujahedins, Muslim holy warriors. The building shook. We were afraid and pleased at the same time. We knocked on the door so the guards would let us out into the corridor, but they had run to take shelter in the cellar like cowards, and they locked us in our rooms and left us there. Because of the danger, we broke the door down and ran to the cellar, where we found those "brave" Muslims, like mice in a hole, who are only brave when they beat camp inmates who can't and don't dare defend themselves. The shells fell on the roof of the building, which caused it to shake again. I saw Saka at last, and we talked a little.

Saturday, September 12, 1992

We work all day long. We clean the rooms and corridors, fix the roof of the damaged building, and above all this we dig the trenches. We collapse from the fatigue. We are hungry, and we have to work.

Sunday, September 13, 1992

Work on the roof and digging of trenches. Nadil released to go home.

As the room leader I had to write a thank you note to the camp management because they "evacuated us to the cellar during the shelling." Risto Cvijetić suggested I do this, on Hamzić's orders. I knew what was in store if I refused: I would be beaten again.

I found out today from "Z" that the refugees will be moved to my house from the school in Donje Moštre. I have no idea who they are, from where they come and how many people are there. I only know that the fact hit me very deeply. Is this the way to make a democratic, civil and modern country, based on international principles? Is this a just way to treat a man who was against Srpska demokratska stranka—SDS (Serbian Democratic Party) politics and their followers? The fact is that in this land, we have to exist and live together. Wasn't it enough that they had robbed my house and carried away my TV set, recorder, radio, two sets of dishes, Zepter, knives, microwave oven, car, firewood, all clothes, dishes and crystal vases, and even small things like the hairdryer, mixers, calculators, cameras, sport shoes and many other things? Is this my reward for being loyal (I was indeed) and living in a country like this? Who am I to ask for help and protection? My neighbors? No . . . by no means.

How can I ask them that, when it was they who demolished the door of my house several times and took away all my belongings from my house—the things that my wife and I had bought by saving our money? Turn to the police station? How can I turn to them when they made it possible for my neighbors to carry out whatever they wanted? They didn't do anything to prevent this. No, there is nobody to ask for help. Wouldn't it have been more honest to let me go home after all I have suffered these ninety days, and then to ask me to receive the refugees? After all, these people didn't leave their home willingly, and they aren't at fault for this meaningless war. Is there any humanity or honesty left in the human race? Is it fair to expel a man from his own home for no other reason than that he is a Serb? And where am I to go tomorrow when they tell me I am free? Where? Why? No . . . I really don't know.

> Where to go? I myself don't know
> For in my home other people dwell;
> From this camp somehow out I'll go
> But my despair is a bottomless well.
> I built my house with my own hands,
> My children played at the river banks;
> With my wife I had a happy life
> But the whirl of war destroyed it all.
> Shall I be allowed to enter my house,
> Have a drink and sleep with a smiling face?
> Will they let me linger about
> And admit me to my own place?

[In order to prove that the guards took care of us, and that they took us to shelter during the shelling, I had to write a thank you note to the camp administration, which was signed by all the camp inmates. It was then shown on TV in Visoko that we were thanking our torturers for caring for us and saving our lives.]

Monday, September 14, 1992

The warden Zijo takes me to Hamzić and Mrčo–but even he doesn't know why. We arrive downstairs and Mrčo takes a wooden baton and starts hitting me. I cannot defend myself because of the cast on my arm. The warden cannot watch; he tries to leave the room, but Hamzić doesn't allow him to leave. Mrčo hits me on the head with the baton and kicks me in the stomach, genitals, shinbones. He beats me because of the storage heater that exploded in my house. Somebody turned it on and when it warmed up it exploded because I had hidden my gun, bullets and a bomb in there, long before the arrest.

Because of the pain, I try to jump out of the window, but Mrčo grabs me by my shirt and keeps beating me. After about twenty minutes he stops on the pleading of the warden, who takes me to the toilet and washes my face. I ask him for a gun to kill myself because I can't bear it any longer. He doesn't give it to me, and he takes me to my room. Luka and Zdravko treat my wounds again, and the warden gives me some pills for the pain.

Tuesday, September 15, 1992

I didn't sleep last night. I had to sit up because my head was swollen and hurt. My ear went blue, and my shins were also in pain. The others look at me encouragingly to tell me to hold on and endure all this humiliation and physical torture. I will endure. I will surely endure, as they can never kill the pride and humanity in each of us. We can be blue and hungry and broken up and thirsty, but there will still remain that Serbian pride in us. I shall endure.

Wednesday, September 16, 1992

They did not beat me yesterday, but today. . . ? It seems they won't today. The pain subsides a little. Zijo calls me out into the corridor to tell me that it seems that Mrčo ran away after beating me up. I suppose he realized it was a hopeless lost cause and nothing would come from it. For a moment I forget about the pain and feel somehow proud and joyful.

Thursday, September 17, 1992

Fish for breakfast—one can for the three of us. Luka and Zdravko quarrel about the can opener—a trifle. A peaceful day. Visiting day. Tina came to see Luka, and Zdravko also went out. While I write in the diary, they cover for me and watch out so no one can see me.

Friday, September 18, 1992

Mother and Mother-in-law came. Brought lots of food. We talked about how the heating stove had exploded in my house. A policeman from Goražde had moved in and after the explosion, he took everything he liked from the house and went on. But it doesn't matter now. Just to have enough food and to reach Serbian territory somehow. This is all that matters.

Saturday, September 19, 1992

Nurija and Dževad—investigating judges—came to talk

about the explosion. Gave me cigarettes. They will come tomorrow also for an additional statement from me.

> [I was lied to by Hamzić and Mrčo on Sept. 14th 1992 that three people died during this explosion, when in fact no one was killed. A TV crew came to film that event. I lied that I had nothing to do with it, but that some of the robbers must have planted the explosives.]

Sunday, September 20, 1992
Mentally relieved at last. I finished the statement. I did not dare admit that I had planted the bombs and the rest. They tried to catch me in a lie by cross-examining me, but failed. They lack the qualifications to do this job.

Monday, September 21, 1992
Finally someone is to leave the camp. About fifteen old and ill people sent home. Among them are Veljko Milanović, Milan Kačar, Djordjo Cvijetić, Ilija Panić, Bogdan Spasojević and others. Fine—there is more space in the room now and the mood is better. Everyone thinks that they will be the next to go home.

Tuesday, September 22, 1992
Bogdan Spasojević came back all black and blue (he is a mental patient). Someone beat him up in the night in Grančanica when he was going home. In the afternoon Senad Dedić—a guard from the camp, who is also a neighbour of his—took him home.

Wednesday, September 23, 1992
Another shock today—Željo Bajić went out to work and saw Mrčo. After seven days, fear is spreading again. It seems that he did not succeed in running away. I talk to Željo and Mike Bajić.

Thursday, September 24, 1992
Visiting day. Mrčo came into the dormitory just to scare us. Mother-in-law came. Zoran Krsmanović got beaten up just

before the visit and everyone saw him blue. The visit is over. Everybody is eating what was brought to them. Vlajko, Stame, Rajcin, Željo, Mike, Neno and I sit at the table. Mike is smoking and telling us that he told Nela to bring his sons to see him. At 7:25 p.m. a dumdum bullet comes through the window. We lie down even though it is dark. Mike Bajić cries, "I am hit!" Željo starts shouting, "Mike, Mike!" A stream of blood from his neck. We bang on the door. No one opens it. Finally they open it and we carry him out into the corridor. He is dead. He has bled to death and died in Željo's arms. No one is sleeping because of the shock. The shrapnel hit Vlajko, Neno and Davor, and me in the hip. A crazy night.

Friday, September 25, 1992

The morning resembles a dream—a nightmare. We clean the blood from the room after Mike's death. Željo cries the whole night and morning. "Experts" come to the room. Milan Petrović and another one claim that the bullet came from Čekrčići— genuine ballistics. We are bitter.

The visit of my mother-in-law. Talks of Visoko being shelled and damaged. Joco Milanović transferred from Visoko prison to a correctional institution in Zenica. Visit over. We are again sitting around tables. All of a sudden, strong detonations. A grenade hits under the window and a pane falls down, hitting Rajko Milanović, called Rajcin, on the head. The room is full of smoke, dust, fear. Everybody lying down on the floor. We bang on the door, but no one opens. Another strong detonation. A grenade flies into Room 4 and hits the wall half a meter above Rade Krsmanović's head. We break open the door and go out into the corridor. Slobodan Lero and Nenad Vanovac burst out of Room 4. Smoke comes out through the door. Dušan Nikolić also comes out, blood all over his face. People are running down the stairs to the cellar. We carry out Nikola Šarenac, who is wounded in the left leg. Cousin Jovo is well, I see, but hit in the arm, and blood is flowing down his fingers. I find out that Milo Krunić is already dead and Trivo badly wounded. After all the wounded have been transferred to the health centre, we stay in the cellar. Eighteen people have been wounded and Milo Krunić is dead. Milorad Stojančević also wounded in the shoulder and back by shrapnel. Zoran Krsmanović also wounded. In the evening they take us from the cellar to Rooms 5, 6 and 7 looking over Visoko, not Čekrčići.

Saturday, September 26, 1992

We are cleaning the rooms. TV Visoko comes and films the rooms hit by Chetniks from Ilijaš. Room 4 is full of blood. The walls bullet-riddled. Things, blankets, scattered all around. Windows displaced from their frames. Blood all over the walls. It is impossible to wash and clean the room.

Sunday, September 27, 1992

I am in Room 6 with Luka and Zdravko, Radovan, Saka and the rest. We talk about the last two or three days. The list of killed officially confirmed Trivo and Milo's death and the others out of danger. Nikola Šarenac lost a lot of blood—shrapnel cut his artery in the left thigh.

Monday, September 28, 1992

Roll call again. We are separated now and I am with the members of our headquarters and Mrdić's. Here are Velo, Čorba, Siniša "Cila" Vučenović, Milenko Maleš, Ćićo Damjanović, Rade Krsmanović, Boro Toljević, Brano Ćebo. We are together and prattle about Rooms 5 and 7 being designated for exchange, Room 6 for release by October 1, 1992 as agreed with the Red Cross from Geneva and Phillipe Morillon. We have enough food as Čorba, who distributes food to rooms, is with us.

[The headquarters refers to that which commanded all actions before we were captured. The Mrdić family, I and some others were there. We were the worst "extremists."]

Tuesday, September 29, 1992

The warden takes me out and asks that I make lists by rooms. I go from room to room and talk with everybody. Everyone is hopeful, but Rajcin claims that there will be no releases. According to him, we will get out when our men liberate us by force or at the end of the war. Smart aleck. I visited the wounded also. Jovo operated on and feels better.

[The warden said I should make the list of inmates in alphabetical order.]

Wednesday, September 30, 1992

Red Cross from Geneva came. We told them everything about the deaths. I received a message from Kosta Sikime from Belgrade. I was happy—I sent an answer. On the same day nine people transferred from the cellar to Zenica.

Friday, October 2, 1992

My mother and Vesna came and brought me a lot of food. They say that I look much better now than a month ago. They are fine. They'll send me some pictures from home, the ones that were left, since the plunderers took everything from the house, and the things they didn't like they tore and burned. Today, after a bath, while he was cleaning the corridor, Drago Vanovac from Radovlje got beaten. Domac and Esno beat him. He is all blue on his back, neck and face.

Saturday, October 3, 1992

Attack on our lines on Osijela. Everything shaking and reverberating from detonations. Danger sirens sound as usual before they intend to attack. The attack stopped at noon. It started raining.

[Osijela, a hill above the town of Visoko, overlooking it. This was where the line of separation was.]

Monday, October 5, 1992

An ordinary day. We organize a tournament in games. Čorba won; he first beat Dobro Milić and then Brano Ćebo in the finals.

Wednesday, October 7, 1992

Red Cross is coming. Before that we take the slop-pail

outside so that they do not see it in the room. They ask us about the conditions and treatment. We dare not tell the truth. We only ask if anyone will be let home. They don't know anything either.

Thursday, October 8, 1992

Investigating judges came again to talk about the explosion. Dževad and the commander of state security came in person to check on me. They tried with some kind of cross-examination to catch me in a lie, but they didn't succeed. They gave me a picture of my wife with my daughter Tamara, when she was coming out of the maternity hospital Kosevo in Sarajevo after the birth. They let me go. I go to be shaved. Hasan Karavdić does not know anything new. Mother-in-law and Vesna came.

Friday, October 9, 1992

I don't expect a visit, but they call me out to the room where the guards are. To my surprise, Vesna, my brother-in-law, Stevan, and their daughter Irma have come to see me. Stevan looks good as well as Irma, but he says that the Serbs are not allowed to walk around anywhere and they have to stay in their homes. He gives me some cigarettes and we drink coffee. A real refreshment. Stevo tells me in front of the guards that when I come out of the camp I must go home, and when the guards are not looking, he winks at me to inform me to go anywhere else but not to return home, because there is nothing to return to. Suljo Burko and his guards have eaten the whole sweet pie that Vesna made and brought to me. The insolent motherfuckers.

Monday, October 12, 1992

We play cards—me, Velo, Lav, Rade Šarenac. I am called out into the corridor. Cikota waits for me there. They also call Zoka Krsmanović and Brane Kokoruš. We go down to the ground floor. They first bring in Brane, while Zoka and I wait in the corridor and Mrčo rages in the office. They are beating him. Brane comes out some fifteen minutes later, red in face. Zoka, who is wounded, enters. They beat him too, but less. Probably because he is wounded. He comes out, I go in. Mrčo, Hamzić,

Cikota, Miralem "Čenga" Čengić and another new one inside. Mrčo is sitting. Hamzić stands up and asks, "Who takes drugs here?" He hits me in the chin with his fist. Then everyone hits me with what they can grab hold of and wherever they can get at me. I don't know how, but they throw me around the room like a ball. From the door to the window, under the bed, on the table. Then I am on my back on the floor, and Čengić kicks me in the chest. I feel my ribs breaking. I can't breathe. Mrčo stops them from beating me. I go outside and Cikota takes us to the toilets to wash our faces. Then he sends us back to our rooms, and Cikota hits me in the kidney with his fist as a farewell. Again, pain, fear, bruises, questions of my friends—*why?* Savo Mrdić puts poultices on me. Mladjo is also there. In the evening Senad Dedić plays cards with us and says that the old men will go home in two or three days.

Wednesday, October 14, 1992

Everything still hurts, but a little less. In the afternoon a meeting of military police representatives from Semizovac (Božo Sivac) and Visoko took place in connection with the closing down of the camp. Lav got the brush-off from Pinć. Čorba is distributing the food again. I mostly talk to Mladjo Mrdić.

Thursday, October 15, 1992

Shaving. My back and legs still hurt. Mother, Cmilja and Tina came to visit. Found out that at home our cow was taken away as well as the money father had gotten from selling our calf. They wanted to slaughter him. For six days now the sirens have not sounded.

[They took away the possessions of all the Serbs in Visoko and surrounding area. They took away all my father's money and his livestock and poultry.]

Friday, October 16, 1992

No bath. We are glad because it is cold. The glass on the windows burst from the detonations and nobody fixes it. It is better to be dirty than sick. Lav went to Mrčo for interrogation and he asked arms from him. Fear and uncertainty.

Monday, October 19, 1992

Admir Babić and another man, a gypsy, have been arrested and brought into our room. They smuggled ammunition and arms. We went for firewood. Vlajko's house and barn have been burned down and someone has moved into his new home. We cut down trees for firewood belonging to Vlajko and Cvijetko Jovašević and Voja Ribar. Nenad V. was taken for interrogation in the evening.

Wednesday, October 21, 1992

Suće Herceglija and Hindija Osman were taken away because they had stolen cattle from the Serbs together with Adem Omerbegović, Enes Birno, Nijaz Ajdinović, Salem Zerdo, Nihad Herceglija. Lav got a box of cigarettes from Kemo Smajlović.

Thursday, October 22, 1992

About twenty new prisoners, Serbs, were brought in. Among them Vaso Vanovac, Milenko "Mišo" Topalović, Boško Stojančević, Rada Bajić and Dušanka Stojčić. We found out that Ivica had killed one and wounded another police officer of the Territorial Defense. On that occasion Željo Bajić's uncle from Kakanj was killed. No visits.

Saturday, October 24, 1992

Vaso Vanovac, Tihomir Kokoruš and some others from the other rooms were released home. Thank God that at least someone has left the camp, and my turn will probably come too.

Sunday, October 25, 1992

Finally an exchange takes place. Twenty men are taken to be exchanged at Ilijaš, among them Nikola Šarenac, Slavko Masal, Nedjo Koprivica, Dragan Krstović, Simo Šljivić, and Stamenko and Milenko Krsmanović. Joy because of the departures and new hope.

October 24, 25, 26, 27, 28, 1992

Off to work, cutting down of trees for firewood and a trip to
Visočica. Nothing special.

[Visočica is the mountain that is the symbol of
Visoko and dominates the town. We dug trenches on
its peaks overlooking the Serbian positions in Čekrčići
and Kralupi and were exposed to gun bullets and shell
shrapnel.]

Thursday, October 29, 1992

A visit: mother, Tina, Tankosa, Ljubica and Cmilja. Boro
Toljević got some plum brandy in a candy box. He, Mladjo and
I had a drink. I received my medicine.

[I got medicines from my cousin Rajko Šavija who
was the director of the Visoko pharmacy and sent them
by "Z."]

Friday, October 30, 1992

A visit. Our men are working with timber. Rade Krsmanović
taken for a private exchange at Kiseljak. Afterwards he was
brought back. Lav had to give a statement in connection with
the Deutsche marks he gave for cigarettes.

[It was a private exchange in which the Muslims
were supposed to get about 3,000 German marks.]
[The guards took money from us to buy cigarettes
for us, either at a much higher price or they did not bring
them at all, but kept the money.]

Saturday, October 31, 1992

Alleged date for closing down the camp, but nothing came
of it. Anticipation.

Sunday, November 1, 1992

There is nothing of leaving the camp. I took the cast off my
arm and talked to the doctor. He told me that my arm had healed
fine and that everything would be okay. My relative Jovo, who

was wounded in his left arm during the shell explosion in Room 4, also went for a checkup. They didn't fix his arm well after the injury and he will remain seventy percent disabled in his arm. It seems like the Muslim doctors do not care about that.

November 2, 3, 4, 5, 1992
Daily work in the woods and on the road to Visočica. Nothing came of the closing down of the camp. We found out that Saša and Njonja from Banja Luka have been exchanged.

Friday, November 6, 1992
My mother-in-law and Vesna came and brought me some food. The Muslims almost don't feed us at all any more. We are used as free labor and tortured to their satisfaction. My mother and father are fine, if that's the truth, because they hide things from me like I hide from them so they won't worry.

Saturday, November 7, 1992
We are taken to work every day. We are exhausted and tired, and on top of everything, hungry. We go to Visočica, Čvrsnica, Krtnica, Gornja Zimća. Everyone has to go except the invalids.

Thursday, November 12, 1992
Mother came to visit. I found out that our cow was slaughtered just after being taken out of the barn. That's how real neighbours behave—needless to say. Mom and Dad have decided to leave Muslim territory.

Saturday, November 14, 1992
The first snow has fallen. We thought we wouldn't go to work, but we were mistaken. It is even harder to work now since it is slippery and cold, and we don't have winter clothes and shoes.

Sunday, November 15, 1992
Mrčo came to the dormitory. He told Boro Toljević that he will not leave the camp alive. Fear.

Monday, November 16, 1992

I went to dig trenches over Gorani in the same group with Boško Marić and Milan Kuvać. Muhamed Zukić guarded us.

[Gorani is a hill towards Kiseljak on which there is a mountain cottage. The Muslims were holding that part and we had to dig the trenches there.]

November 17, 1992

Ten of us were digging the trenches on Visočica and on the eastern side towards the Serbian positions. The leaves had fallen and now we could see clearly the Serbian line of trenches. We dug the trench, but it went slowly because the earth was hard and full of rocks. The guard with us was Suljo Burko. We suddenly heard firing from the Serbian side and saw the bullets driving into the ground next to us. We threw the tools and ran to the shelter on the other side of Visočica. We were all terrified, because death was so close. The guard Suljo was the most terrified of all. Because of the fear, he had forgotten to take his rifle, and then he ordered Mrdić Lazo to bring it for him because he didn't dare. A brave guard, no question.

We no longer dug trenches, but we went on foot to the army barracks where the camp was—a forty minute walk. While we were walking through the town of Visoko in a file, I saw familiar surroundings and streets. Next to the post office in Ognjen Prica street there was a huge hole in the asphalt in which a car could fit. A lot of buildings were knocked down and the walls were full of holes from the shell fragments, the windows broken from the detonations. We went by the municipal building where I had worked for more than ten years. Everything was closed, and on the streets were branches, leaves, garbage. We came to the gypsy houses, and they peeped out from their houses and cursed our "Chetnik mothers" and spit on us. That human riffraff was now better to the Muslims than we—the honest citizens and respectable people. Oh my God, what humiliation. It seemed like it now was a gypsy and mujahedin's town. So sad that one could cry.

Thursday, November 19, 1992

Vesna came for a visit. I was transferred to Room 9. Abdulah Hašimović, called Haša, and Nermin Goralija brought in. Ćičko got cigarettes from Haša. The Red Cross came. Asked about Montenegro.

[The International Red Cross was supposed to take some men to Montenegro through an exchange. They wanted to know whether we were willing to go there, as they could not take us to the Serbian territory.]

November 26, 1992 – December 3, 1992

Work and hunger day in, day out, trenches and felling of trees. We fight among ourselves who is to go and cut down trees because there is more to eat there. I heard that my uncle was killed by a shell.

[Uncle had been released and was at home. There was shelling that day and I heard that he had been killed by a shell.]

Friday, December 4, 1992

My mother-in-law and Vesna came to see me. They say that they talked to Siniša, my nephew, in Berlin, and that he said that my wife and children are okay and that they send their greetings. My mother and father are under pressure to move away from the house, since there are a lot of refugees without a home. You have to leave because it doesn't matter if the house is yours, when the country isn't. This is now a Muslim country and there is no room for Serbs in it.

Tuesday, December 8, 1992

Went to Gornja Zimća. Brought eleven liters of grape brandy into the room. The Red Cross came and brought us cigarettes—Ronhil. We had to give a few packs, "voluntarily," to the guards.

Wednesday, December 9, 1992

The guards found the brandy last night, because stupid

Lav and Velo drank too much of it and whistled and shouted in the room as if they were free. We all had to go out of the room into the corridor, and the guards searched our room and found and took away the rest of the brandy. We were fools. But they shouldn't be criticized, since we all crave everything, and who knows if and when we will come out from this place. One does not live here for tomorrow, only for today because tomorrow . . . we don't have tomorrow.

We had luck in all this since the head of the shift of the guards was Sead Kadrić, called Šicko, who was the best of all the guards and he did his job most decently. I have known him from before. He was a tall and strong young man, a karate expert with a black belt, but I believe that not one camp inmate can say that Šicko cursed at him, let alone hit him. I take my hat off to him; there were few like him. Even in bad times, one should not regard everyone as equal; not all the guards were the same. The evil and good should always be separated.

Tuesday, December 15, 1992

The Red Cross came. From our room Panić, Dule Vuković, Neno, Risto "Riki" Cvijetić, Boro Toljević and Milenko Kuvać are going to Montenegro. Altogether, sixty-nine men. Of all the Milanovićs in camp, they arranged for me and Jovo to remain in Visoko—that's super.

Wednesday, December 16, 1992

Šicko's shift again. We smuggled the grape brandy again, but this time there were no problems. The time passes and there are fewer and fewer beatings, and we become more and more relaxed. When we return from work exhausted, the man who takes us to work lets us buy alcohol and cigarettes for ourselves. That man is Sead Habibija, called Sejo, who understands our troubles and has known the majority of us from before. He knows who we are and who we used to be. So we sometimes take the alcohol and that is the only thing that gives us strength to endure all this. I think about everything we have endured so far in the camp. First the plundering of our material goods (at home and in the camp), then physical mistreatment (beatings, hunger, thirst), and then mental mistreatment (fear, humiliation). And now physical exploitation goes on that can only end in religious and cultural extermination. Once upon a time, there used to be a nation . . .

Friday, December 18, 1992

The men should have left for Montenegro but something came up. Everyone is depressed. Now, those who are not on the list for Montenegro have to go and work. Screwed up.

Wednesday, December 23, 1992

Sixty-nine men leave for Montenegro. We watch through the window while they get into the bus. Zijo, the camp warden, and Hamzić are in front of the gate. Everyone said goodbye to Zijo, while only Riki and Jelenko Panić bid Hamzić farewell. From this group only eighteen people went home: Vlajko, Simo, Bato, Stame (all Krsmanovićs), Mile Panić, Luka and Radovan Milanović, and some others. We don't know why they are going home. The Red Cross promised that they would come for us soon. We were moved to different rooms. I am together with Mladjo and Ušljo, nicknamed Vamp.

Friday, December 25, 1992

No visitors either today or yesterday because of the shelling. Found out from Nermin Masnopita that our men arrived at Montenegro and that their arrival was shown on TV. Sejo promised to bring grape brandy tomorrow, three litres for ten Deutsche marks.

December 26-31, 1992

We work daily at Gornja Zimća cutting down trees, expecting the Red Cross and the closing down of the camp. We have no food.

Friday, January 1, 1993

No visits today or yesterday. The commander of the barracks, Fuad Softić, prohibited them. New Year in the camp. I think of my family. We did not go to work today—exemption because of

New Year's Day. Discipline not as strict as it used to be. I bought three liters of grape brandy and a box of Ronhil cigarettes for sixteen Deutsche marks.

January 3, 4, 5, 1993

We are working every day, cutting down trees. We had a chance to run away in the direction of Kiseljak due to the dense fog, but were afraid to because they would take revenge on the others. On January 5, 1993, Mom came to the worksite at Gornja Zimća and brought brandy and meat.

[Many of us thought about running away from Gornja Zimća towards Kiseljak and then to Rakovica where our forces were, but despite the ideal conditions—the fog, darkness, vicinity of Kiseljak (about three kilometers)—we did not dare make up our minds to take such a step because some of those who remained in the camp would certainly be killed.]

Wednesday, January 6, 1993

Christmas Eve. Mrdić, Savo Cvjetić, Velo and I had a few drinks and a bite to eat, the food that mother brought to Zimća yesterday.

Thursday, January 7, 1992

Christmas. Forty-two of us divided into two groups and celebrated Christmas. A small oak tree branch was there. I was with Šarenac and we talked and joked. We toasted and spoke of God. I found out from Vesna yesterday that "Z" sent word that I would be sent home. I am pleased but would prefer to be exchanged. The guards also wished us a merry Christmas. Things have become somewhat more relaxed.

[An oak branch is the symbol of Christianity that is brought into Serb houses at Christmas.]

Saturday, January 9, 1993

Exactly twenty-one days have passed since we had a bath.

We worked in the mud yesterday and are as dirty as pigs. Presumably the Red Cross is coming on Wednesday.

Monday, January 11, 1993

I went to work in the forest. I was carrying a thick tree and due to the ice I slipped, fell down and hurt my broken arm. It hurts terribly.

Tuesday, January 12, 1993

My hand hurts and I am not working. Our men went to dig trenches at Zbilje. The frontline. Drago Vanovac was wounded in the chin. Everyone is full of fear again.

> [They took us—the remaining camp inmates—to the frontline, the so-called "Zbilje," where we dug trenches in the direction of the Serbian lines. Dragomir Vanovac was wounded on that occasion in the chin and Siniša "Cila" Vučenović, (son of Djordje), in the behind.]

Thursday, January 14, 1992

The Red Cross came. We told them we had to dig trenches and that they should do something to protect us. They brought us blankets, soap, detergent, cigarettes and raisins. For the time being, nothing new regarding the closing down of the camp. Today is New Year's Day (Serbian) and last night there were real fireworks at midnight at the frontline. The Serbs were shooting like mad to celebrate New Year's Eve.

Monday, January 18, 1993

The Mrdićs and Tesan were called to go somewhere. Waited for Mladjo because he worked at Gornja Zimća. We don't know where they will go.

Tuesday, January 19, 1993

There aren't many of us left in the camp, only about seventeen. One by one they leave, and when and where will I go? Maybe after we cut and drag off all the wood. Maybe in spring when flowers bloom . . . but then they will need someone to mow the grass. Maybe . . . maybe never.

Thursday, January 21, 1993
Finally visits are permitted again, and my mother, Vesna and mother-in-law came. I found out that Izabela was having a hard time on her own with the children, but my own family is no better off because no one works and there is no money.

Sunday, January 24, 1993
The front in Krajina has opened, which is not good for the Serbs. Croats and Muslims are fighting against each other in Vakuf and the road from Zenica to Visoko is blocked at Lašva. Everything is against us. Nothing will come of the exchange. Our men are working in the trenches at Zbilje and we are pulling down the prison walls and building a hospital.

Monday, January 25, 1993
Lav got drunk and screwed up on the brandy. They have now interrogated even Sejo, who let us buy it. We all had to go out to the corridor so the guards could search the rooms. I was afraid that they would find my diary. Lav was a real idiot. Even that little pleasure will be denied to us now because of him. During the trench digging on Zbilje, Cila was wounded in his rear. Who knows what will happen next time.

Tuesday, January 26, 1993
In the same building with Fahrudin Jamaković and Žućo because they have deserted, too, and are confined. Dule Vuković came for some kind of certificate from the camp authorities.

[Their deserters and our former neighbors were shut up in the same room with us. That is what happened to Fahrudin Jamaković and Salem Zerdo, nicknamed Žućo.]

Thursday, January 28, 1993
My mother came to visit. We had a long talk. She told me that Milenko Duvnjak came out of Zenica and that the Mrdićs are in Zenica. Velo sprained his knee in the trenches and it

became swollen. Provocations and shooting in Kalotići. I made arrangements with Mother that in case I was released they should leave immediately for Kiseljak and then from Rakovica to Ilijaš. Visoko is blocked from all sides.

Friday, January 29, 1993
Visits. We have food. Velo and I were called together to the hearing of Lav and some others—assumed they were going home. No one is very happy to go home. Everyone would prefer to be part of an exchange. It is clear to everyone that there is no return to where we once lived.

Saturday, January 30, 1993
Since the morning we have been working in the cellar. We break down the walls, hungry, in the dust. At noon, the warden comes and reads the names of the camp inmates who are to be exchanged to Ilijaš. Through an empty room, the names resound . . . Jovo Marić, Radoja Krsmanović, Brano Lukić, Drago Vanovac, Dušan Nikolić . . . then he stops as if that is all and as if he is about to leave, and after a few minutes, as long as an eternity, he smiles, and a sound like the most beautiful bells resounds in the room, ". . . and Skot." Skot is my nickname, given to me in primary school by a teacher because I played football sharply and fast like a Scottish player. The name echoes through the room, ". . . and SKOT . . . and SKOT."

I feel dizzy. I have tears in my eyes and my legs begin to shake as if I will fall down. I couldn't believe it. Like in a delirium, we go to our rooms and pack our things, although we have nothing to pack besides the things the International Red Cross has brought to us. We say goodbye to everyone who remains in the camp, wishing that they leave as soon as possible and that God help them endure. They are also glad that we leave because they hope they will be next. I say goodbye to my relative Jovo, who is the last Milanović in the camp, with a promise that we will see each other again in freedom.

I take my things and a jacket. Only after I take it in my hands do I begin to feel afraid. What should I do? Wrapped inside the jacket is everything we have survived and that we must not forget—the things everyone should know about—THE DIARY. We go out to the corridor, where the warden and army policemen are. I ask him to go to the toilet. He allows it. I stand in the toilet with the diary in my hands, hesitating, trying to decide whether to destroy it or to smuggle it with me to freedom. Freedom is so close and the diary is the only thing that stands between it and myself. Is it worth risking my life to show people what we experienced in Visoko and at whose hands? I am at the edge of an abyss. Freedom or death?

After what seems to me a long pondering, I decide to keep the diary and try to smuggle it. I cannot so easily forget or dismiss everything we have lived through in Visoko. The guard calls me out to the corridor. I am afraid. The others are standing against the wall with their arms and legs spread apart. The guards are frisking them. I am standing next to Jovo Marić at the end of the line. The policeman who is in charge of searching me is talking with the warden about something, and the others urge him to hurry. I watch Jovo with his legs spread apart and with his pockets turned out, his shoes off. *What will happen to me?* I think, as beads of perspiration appear on my forehead. The other policemen have almost finished the search and they hurry the one who is talking to the warden. Fortunately for me, he only searches my pockets, my trousers and shoes because he has no time. When he turns me around he sees that I am covered in sweat and asks me what is wrong with me. I somehow, almost without sound, manage to say that I was ill last night with a temperature, and that today we worked hard in the cellar all day long, so I am sweating because of this. To this he sarcastically replies that I will be healed by "my Chetniks" in Ilijaš. Fortunately, he is right, and this is how my diary and I survive.

At 12:30 we leave for the exchange, which is scheduled to occur in Župča, a settlement between Ilijaš and Breze. We sit in a Muslim army police van along with two policemen. Nobody says anything, and our hearts beat as if they will jump out of our chests with joy. We are not exchanged until 5:30 p.m., when we are led single file by a Serbian member of the exchange commission onto Serbian territory. Walking by the Serbian military truck I see the Serbs throwing out the corpses of the Muslims who died in the fight with the Serbs. It reminds me of how we, the camp inmates, threw logs onto the trucks for them. Now we throw their dead like logs. The truck is full of them.

Finally, I am in Serbian territory. Many of our family and friends are waiting for the six of us. Everybody is happy for each Serb who enters Serbian territory. Around us are bearded Serbs with cartridge belts across their shoulders and machine guns in their hands. I feel like I am flying. *FREEDOM at last.*

A bearded man in a fur hat with a cockade on it appears in front of me, and he is crying. Only after he begins to laugh with tears in his eyes do I recognize my relative Ljuban, who is one of the only Milanovićs who left everything and went to Ilijaš before the war began. He asks me how I am, but I cannot answer. We only hug each other and cry together. I am the happiest person in the world, although I cannot see anything because of the tears.

There will always be reminders, but I will never forget.

How I Wrote My Diary

While I was kept prisoner in the camp of Visoko, I saw a new, dark face of humankind, a face that was unknown to me and completely different from the one I used to see. I cannot explain or find justification for all the evil and mistreatment we had to endure for the sole reason that we were Christians (Serbs) and not of Islamic religion (Muslims). Often, very often, while I was prisoner in the Visoko camp, from June 20, 1992, on, I thought about everything that was happening to us and tried to find a reason for why it all happened. I asked myself whether it was really such a sin to be a Serb, and so terrible a sin that because of it we had to endure all that pain in order to survive. I felt this especially because it all happened in our native town where we had lived all our lives and where we had socialized with all people and had made friends regardless of their religion or nationality.

All Serbs had numerous friends among the Muslims (In Visoko about 80% of the population were Muslims), many of whom forgot overnight that they were our friends. They turned their backs on us, not attempting to help us in any way. When you had to enter the camp, you would encounter well-known faces, but you would see them on the opposite side of the prison bars. They had been our guards. We expected that when all this came to an end they would release us to go freely where we wanted. They didn't tell us, though, that we would not be allowed to return to our homes, because our homes had become theirs. It was now their Islamic state, where naturally we had no place. And worst of all, those who held us prisoner were our well-known colleagues from work, neighbors, players from the same soccer teams, acquaintances and schoolmates. A former friend and the chief of the camp was our former teacher of mathematics. Hard to imagine they would beat us, give us no water or bread, extinguish their cigarettes on our hands, rob us and finally shoot us.

It seems that for a long time we had kept our eyes shut and didn't notice what was going to happen. Arriving at this ominous camp, our eyes opened very soon. With the first beating we saw what those less "guilty" had to endure. We asked ourselves what would happen to those "more" guilty—namely those who insisted more strongly on being Serbs, because in the camp the so-called "guilt" was estimated by the degree to which one expressed his Serbian identity. We suffered from beatings that even the old and sick men endured, even children, young men aged sixteen to eighteen.

My uncle, Miloš Milanović, was over sixty and was a teacher of Serbian, Russian and French languages. When for the third time in two days he was beaten by his former pupils, I was unable to listen anymore to his screaming and weeping. He entered the room crying as a little child, and he had bruises all over his arms, back, neck, legs. Blood was leaking from the wounds on his head. We both cried, as it was all that we found soothing. I didn't know what to do; I tried to find the words to calm him, but I was unable to utter a word. He opened his soul to me as somebody knowing that he was going to die, telling me that he would be killed and that he couldn't bear it anymore. He, who had devoted all his life to books, never being interested in politics—how was it possible to accuse him of being a sniper? Because of his poor eyes he had not even been drafted! He wasn't capable of watching TV at a distance beyond seven to eight meters. What an absurdity and what a reason for beating him! He asked me, if I was ever to be released from the camp, to look for Risto Djogo or some other journalist and to tell them what was going on at the camp of Visoko. He asked me also to give a title to such an article, "Bestial Death" or "Slow Dying." With this diary I am fulfilling my promise, hoping that he will have the opportunity to read it and be satisfied.

From that day on, I kept my diary, noting briefly the most important details of the day. I was marking places, names and events in a few words because I had to think of what would happen if I was caught with all the names of the criminals and details on the beatings, starvation and fear. All these paper scraps I hid in an old jacket—I made a hole in the lining through which I pushed the pieces of paper. I think that in those moments I was unaware of the danger I was exposing myself to by writing this diary, and that this would cost me my life if I was accidentally caught with it. In the beginning, I had trustworthy assistants who would hide me while I was writing, watching so that nobody could see me. Those were my uncles, Luka and Zdravko Milanović, and when they were released, Mladjo Mrdić, Velibor Toplanovic, Jovo Marić and Boban Vojnović. On one occasion, I was almost caught when Mrčo suddenly burst into the room and asked me what I was writing. I don't know how, but I managed to slip my bits of paper into the envelope intended for the Red Cross messages, so I answered him that I would send news to my family through the Red Cross. He was looking into the message on my lap, but fortunately, he didn't open it. He only swore my mother and left the room. All the people in the room including myself sighed with relief.

On January 30, 1993, when we were to be exchanged for the Muslim war prisoners from Župča (a village between Ilijaš and Breza), I was wondering whether to destroy my diary or to try to smuggle it with me to freedom. I didn't know if it was worthwhile to risk my life trying to save this diary in order to show people what the Serbs at Visoko had endured and from whom. After a long hesitation, I decided to try to smuggle my diary, but I cannot describe the fear I felt then as I watched the others being searched. By some miracle, I was able to escape with my diary undiscovered.

We started for the exchange, which was to be made at noon, but we were not exchanged until 5:30 p.m. I learned the reason for the delay from Biljana Ćulum, a member of the commission from Ilijaš. The problem was that they were exchanging corpses as well as live prisoners. The commission for the exchange from Ilijaš had brought forty Muslims who had perished in the battle at the mount of Vela, but there were only three Serbian corpses to exchange.

I wish to mention that in the beginning there were other camp prisoners who were taking notes, too, but some of them were discovered and were beaten, and everything they possessed was confiscated. Some others, frightened, threw away their precious notes, which would today be of great personal and historical value.

After I left the camp, I arranged all my notes in chronological order, but I was unable to publish them because a small number of Serbs mentioned in this diary remained at Visoko. By publishing this diary I would jeopardize their lives. Once all concerned were in free Serbian territory and I could not endanger anybody's life, I decided to present to the world what Serbs had endured at Visoko simply because they were Serbs.

By chance I got in contact with Dr. Momčilo Mitrović, who accepted the idea of preparing and printing this book, and as the result of several months of work this book appeared under the title *Muslim's Camp at Visoko 1992-93*.

Now when I read lines from my diary, I see that there were many other things and events worth noting, which passed unnoted because of the specific conditions in which this diary was kept. I should have said much more about health, food and medical assistance; drawn portraits of camp dwellers; described some tragicomic events, and made many other observations.

Health

Life in the camp was lived in abnormal conditions. Room 3, in which we were locked, was seventeen by seven meters, or 119 square meters, and there were 157 camp inmates in the room. It meant that we had less than one square meter for each of us. We slept on the wooden floor, and under our heads instead of cushions we had shoes that we had been wearing all day while digging trenches, going to the lavatory. As we were prisoners during the summer season, we had on light clothes, T-shirts and jeans. While sleeping on the floor we all got bruises on our hips, shoulders, knees. Our clothes were extremely dirty and covered with blood because we had been beaten in those same clothes—we had been sweating in them, wearing them for digging trenches, cleaning garbage and sleeping and had no possibility of washing them.

In spite of such bad conditions, we had our first bath thirty-six days after we were taken prisoner. Our first bath, if one could call it a bath, was on July 25, 1992. Fifty camp inmates were taken into the showers and we had five minutes to use them. In those five minutes, the person in charge of the showers was playing with the switches, letting go, then stopping the cold water, so that some of us got burns from hot water. So a shower was another opportunity for guards to have fun mistreating us. We had no soap, shampoo or clean clothes, so after bathing we would put on the same dirty clothes, spreading dirt all over our bodies again. But that day was for us at least the first opportunity to wash our faces and feel the water on them. Toothbrushes and toothpaste were for us a dream.

We all lived under the same conditions regardless of age, sickness or general health condition. The wounded people had the same life: Dejan Mičanović had wounds on both arms (he is now seventy percent handicapped in his right hand); Gojko

Duvnjak was wounded in the upper right arm, while his clavicle was broken (he is now totally handicapped in his right hand). Old men aged seventy to eighty and men with contagious diseases were living under the same conditions. There was Slavko Topalović, who was operated on for cancer before the war and who died at Derventa after leaving the camp; Slavko Koprivica, who suffered from diabetes and to whom I was giving insulin injections and who died after leaving the camp; Branivoj Radulović, nicknamed Zane, who had tuberculosis; Kačar Milan, who suffered from schizophrenia; Bogdan Spasojević, who was a mentally disturbed person; and many other sick men. Then there were other men who had been beaten and for whom the sole remedy we could provide was wet compresses soaked in the little available water.

As the guards wouldn't allow us to go to the lavatory during the night, a container for urine was placed near the door for all 157 of us in Room 3. It was a can, which could contain about twenty liters, and it was used for urination but also sometimes for defecation. Many, many times during the night, but also in the daytime, the can was overloaded, its content overflowing onto the floor where men were sitting or sleeping. Very often our guards—upon opening the door, when the stench would strike them—were angry with us and would simply kick the can, and the contents would then flow all over the floor. We had to clean it, but the wooden floor had become soaked all through and the stench persisted. That can was only taken out of the room when the International Red Cross was visiting us. Of course we were not free to speak a word about it because we would be punished afterward. Almost regularly when the guard Dizdar was on duty he would kick the can and later, when bringing bread for lunch, in a soldier's dirty blanket, he would throw down the bread on the floor—and we would eat every bit of it.

We had no possibility of washing dishes and they were always dirty. One dish was used by three or four camp inmates in the same room. Somebody from another room had already eaten from that same dish, or would later. We had no forks or spoons; we ate with our fingers or straight from the bent dish. As time passed, our nails grew long and we used them as forks when, by chance, a piece of meat was in the dish. We received our first soap after the second visit of the International Red Cross. For many of us that cake of soap lasted several months as we had no water and the only opportunity to wash our clothes was during bath time, so you had to make up your mind whether, once a month, you should wash your clothes or wash yourself. There wasn't enough time for both. We got towels only when the first visits were allowed, and our visitors brought them for us. Before, after taking a bath, without drying yourself, you would simply put on a dirty T-shirt, which would stick to your body.

Taking into account all these facts, conditions in which we were living, and health conditions of the camp inmates, it is interesting to mention that nobody fell sick from a long-lasting or serious disease, such as leprosy, typhoid fever, mange, or from a less serious disease such as influenza, toothache (with exception of Bogdan Milanović) or from any other disease whatsoever.

The Camp

The Muslim camp for Serbs at Visoko began in April 1992, when Serbs were under investigation in Visoko and the village of Kula Banjer. The camp was situated in the former Yugoslav Army barracks, at the crossing of the streets Oslobodilačkih Brigada and Vladimira Nazora, and opposite the bus station of Visoko. Beside the camp, there was a Croatian monastery. Those were very old buildings, made of hard material with high ceilings and wooden floors. They were used before as bedrooms for Yugoslav National Army soldiers. Rooms 2, 3 and 4 were facing east in the direction of the settlement Čekrčići, which was the separating line between Muslim and Serbian territories. By beeline, the distance between our rooms and Serbian positions was about 500-600 meters. Muslims wanted to reach Sarajevo from Visoko, and to occupy the whole of this territory, but between Visoko and Sarajevo there were Serbian lands and territories in the communities of Ilijaš, Semizovac, Vogošća and Hadžici.

At the separation line between Visoko and Ilijaš there were fights going on almost every day and at the camp we were listening to and watching detonations and fire from all sorts of weapons. Although Muslims outnumbered Serbs, they never managed during the war to break through that line or to move farther in the direction of Sarajevo, because the Serbs were far better soldiers and had better technical equipment. The Muslims were helped by Mudjahidins from Islamic countries. Among them was Osama bin Laden, the well-known Islamic Mudjahidin and terrorist. In those battles, tens of thousands of Muslims were killed and the number of wounded and invalids would eventually be known in the future.

Although Muslims didn't succeed in occupying Serbian territories during the war, they succeeded when the war was over, when the International community headed by the USA, England and Germany attributed key Serbian lands between Visoko and Sarajevo to the Muslims under the Dayton agreement. Now there are no Serbs there at all. Muslims purposely located camps near the frontline, knowing that Serbs from the outside could see us in the camp, so they would abstain from firing or shooting at camp inmates. That is why almost every day they would place rifles aimed at Serbian positions in front of the camp building. We would watch bullets strike the Serbs and the Serbs would not fire back because the Muslims were protected by us, a live shield. Probably because of the cowardice and meanness of the Muslims, the Serbs became infuriated and had to fire back on September 11, 1992. Bombs were falling between the barracks and the earth was shaking. We thought our end was near. By chance, only two bombs struck the roof of the building and nobody was hurt, but the Muslims experienced great fear. In the next few days, we, the camp inmates, repaired the roof of the building, but what was important was that the Muslims stopped firing in front of the building in order to provoke the Serbs. The UNHCR (the UN refugee agency) pointed out to them that they should defend us, liberate us, or transfer the camp.

As Serbian territory was so close, many times we thought of organizing an escape. However, we didn't know what was going on on the other side, as we heard that on the Serbian side everything was covered with mortar shells as a kind of protection against Muslim attacks. We were afraid that freedom would mean death for us, so we abandoned the idea of escape. The only hope we had was the exchange of war prisoners through UNHCR. Therefore, only our dreams were free, while our bodies remained enslaved, having to endure human suffering.

The Muslim camp for Serbs at Visoko remained at the same place till the end of 1994, when the last prisoners were transferred from the camp of Zenica (before the war this was the prison for criminals, during the time President Tito was in office in the former Yugoslavia). Alija Izetbegović was kept prisoner for having written the book *Islamic Declaration*. In that book, he insisted on his Islamic identity and on the continuation of Islamic propagation in Yugoslavia, and that is why he was condemned as a nationalist and kept prisoner in Zenica. Now during the civil war in Bosnia and Herzegovina, that same man was supposed to be the president (for Christians, too: Serbs and Croatians).

The last Serbs in the community of Visoko were exchanged for war prisoners and released to their homes during 1995. Consequently, some of them were prisoners for three full years. This is the story of Serbs from Visoko. Visoko is now ethnically cleansed; now only Muslims live there.

Food

Maybe the worst chapter in the history of the Visoko camp was the food. In the beginning, when we were just taken prisoner, we had three meals a day of a good quality food with sufficient meat. At that time it was the period of the Muslim religious holiday Kurban Bairam, when the Muslims slaughter sheep and beef, and, according to their religious custom, offer the meat to their neighbors. As we were in the camp, a big quantity of meat was delivered to the kitchen where meals for the Muslim army were prepared and we received the same food. At that time, from June 20 until July 8, nobody could complain about the food.

However, as one bad fortune never comes alone, after July 8 we encountered a new one. The Muslims' deceitful policy came to daylight in what happened after the first exchange of war prisoners from the neighboring Serbian community of Ilijaš. Those lucky ones who were first exchanged went to Ilijaš and declared that they had no bad treatment at the Visoko camp and that they had food in abundance. After the impression was given to the media and people that circumstances in the prison camp weren't so bad, that's when the mistreatments began. Breakfast and dinner were abolished without any explanation whatsoever. Camp inmates complained and asked the guards for an explanation, but they were beaten. After that, for breakfast and dinner it was the beating and for lunch the food, which tasted very bad. The quantity was also cut down and from a soldier's dish normally intended for one person, three camp inmates had to eat, while the cover of the dish served one camp inmate. The choice was limited to rice and broad beans with one piece of bread large as a small finger. When bread was distributed, all rushed to grab the heels of a loaf of bread, as they were somewhat larger.

There was general hunger. Men tried to save bits of bread overnight so that they became harder, so they could eat them the next day for breakfast, as hard bread was more satisfying. So the time was passing and we became increasingly hungry, and thinner. Every day men rose from the floor where they slept and headed for the window to breathe a little fresh air. Some made just one pace or two and collapsed from exhaustion. The agony continued. Men were losing weight at a frightening speed. We almost stopped going to the bathroom, as there was no need. We had the can in our room, nobody went to the hall to use the WC, and that suited our guards perfectly. We didn't ask for water because who would drink water when only hungry? Reconciled to our fate, we were expecting to die. Slow dying at the Visoko camp was in progress. However, as time would tell, death didn't come from hunger or thirst, but from shells, bullets, knives and beatings.

Though exhausted and feeble, we were ordered to dig trenches inside the barracks as presumably an attack from Ilijaš was expected—an attack that never happened. We were promised that those who were working would get extra food and water. Men hearing about food would get up unwillingly and go to work. So the first day the working group got to eat and drink as much as they could; they even had water to wash their faces and socks. And so, full and happy, they returned to their rooms after at least one day in prison that wasn't that bad. The next day men started eagerly to work. Twenty men only were selected to work. However, they were not as lucky as the previous group; it was the second day, the day of paying back. To begin, they were all lined up and everything they possessed with them was confiscated: money, watches, bracelets, rings, shoes, simply everything that our torturers found suitable. Then they were forced to dig. Men dug in a channel and guards would pass by, beating prisoners if they found their work unsatisfactory. Some men were taken back to the room unable to walk because they were beaten and exhausted. They didn't even think of asking for food, as beating was given instead of food.

And so every day was different from the previous one, because you didn't know whether you would eat or be beaten.

One would take the risk of being beaten hoping to receive a piece of bread or fruit, anything to eat. There were many heavy smokers in the camp who suffered from the lack of cigarettes. Some of them collected chestnut leaves, dried them, and then made cigarettes using newspaper or toilet paper. There's no end to man's inventive mind. On the occasion of the second visit of the International Red Cross from Geneva, we received soap and cigarettes. For smokers it was the most precious gift. Guards then entered our room bringing fresh, still hot and crunchy bread, saying they would exchange one loaf of bread for three packs of cigarettes. Of course, the nonsmokers eagerly accepted this deal. I think that was the most delicious bread I ever ate in my life. We were happy. The guards of course were satisfied as they sold us the bread, which was due to us, and in exchange, they got a large quantity of cigarettes.

Every day without food was difficult, but I think that one of the most difficult days for us was when visitors from our homes were first allowed to come and bring us food. It was August 14, 1992, when I was asked to come into the hall as my mother had come to visit me. A room with tables placed in the center, dividing the room in two halves, was selected for visits. On one side sat parents, wives, family; on the other the camp inmates. In between, mountains of food were on the table. The nicest food in the world.

In the beginning those visits were allowed once a week, then once in fifteen days. All food remaining after the visits was thrown out by the guards because it was made with pork meat or with pork grease, and according to the Islamic law called Sharia (based on the Koran), they were not permitted to eat anything containing pork. They threw it around the garbage containers; the day after they would bring camp inmates to clean the mess and put the food into the garbage containers. We were hungry and we were forced to throw that food away, and we were not allowed to eat it, because there were always by our side two or three torturers ready to beat us. Then the tears would come unwillingly to our eyes because what we had to endure the animals could not. Only man can suffer such humiliations, and such humiliations can only be imposed by one man to another.

The story told by Ostoja Milanović (son of Mijo) is quite

interesting. He was a prisoner during the Second World War from 1941 to 1945 and was kept in the German camp of Slezen in Poland, where, he said, he had more food than he had in the camp of Visoko. In Slezen he was given one fifth of a loaf of bread, two large boiled potatoes and enough water for the whole day, and at Visoko he was left without food for several days, although he was an elderly man, over seventy-five. He had the misfortune to survive two camps, but he died two years after leaving the camp of Visoko.

One proof of how poorly we were fed is that men didn't go regularly to the lavatory; some of them didn't feel the need for thirty days, while, for instance, Dragan Marković didn't use lavatory for a whole sixty-three days. The majority of the prisoners weighed barely fifty kilograms (seventy to seventy-five pounds). Whether this would have health consequences in the post-camp life of the prisoners, one could only guess.

Medical Care

It surely cannot be said that it was humane to keep men prisoner, to starve them, to torture them physically and mentally, to separate them from their families, to kill them. Besides all I had to live through, I was also exposed to the most inhumane torture, and it was at the level of medical assistance. In fact, for all the people needing medical care—and there were many—"medical assistance" meant the most severe punishment. Two wounded men, Dejan Mičanović and Gojko Duvnjak, were the first to experience it. The day when we were taken prisoner in the camp of Visoko, on June 20, 1992, they were wounded. They were taken away to "receive medical assistance" but were beaten instead, and no medical assistance whatsoever was offered to them. Without any other sanitary material available, we tore our T-shirts and wrapped their arms, just to stop the bleeding. In the following seven days, we didn't remove the improvised bandages, and the wounds became infected. After our intervention with the chief of the camp, he invited a doctor from the Health Center of Visoko to examine the wounded and seriously ill men. I took Dejan out of our room into the next room where the physician was, and when he removed the bandage from his arm I smelled the most disgusting stench I ever smelled in my life. A bullet had passed through his right arm, entered his left arm, and had remained there under the skin. The doctor had to go to the health center to take out the bullet with surgical instruments and to put a bandage on.

It was the same case with Gojko Duvnjak, and with others. All who needed to receive treatment at the health center were afraid to go because they knew they would be beaten.

On July 17, 1992, one group of camp prisoners was digging trenches in the area between the barracks. The Muslims had removed all their guards, and then they threw a shell in the vicinity of the place where camp inmates were working. Nine prisoners were wounded; three of them with serious wounds were transferred to Zenica, while the remaining six were offered medical assistance at Visoko. As was the case with Dejan and Gojko, they were first mistreated and beaten, and only then was medical assistance offered. None among them dared to come again for bandages to be changed, and some of them still carry fragments of shells in their bodies, including Saša Z. Milanović.

I also had a very bad experience going to the health center for medical care, when my arm was broken and swelled, and I needed to go for an x-ray. I was transported with Rade Terzić, and Vojno Raković and accompanied by the chief of the camp and a soldier. It was a bit of luck in this misfortune that the chief of the camp was with me, as he defended me from those who wanted to beat me—I was only exposed to swearing and insults. For all these reasons and because of the lack of medicine, many camp inmates died or were handicapped after leaving the camp. Their deaths were at least partly due to the lack of medical care.

Smoking

Heavy smokers suffered much, lacking cigarettes in the camp. They seemed to tolerate the lack of food better than the lack of cigarettes. As we used to gather in groups of ten to fifteen people, we all smoked together, sitting in a circle, sharing one single cigarette, each of us taking one or two drags. Lucky was the one who got the cigarette in the second round, while the one before him had lips almost burnt trying to finish the cigarette. When smoking in the night, the cigarettes were shining in the dark as sparks. A cigarette had no time to burn down because men smoked so quickly. The ash was long—up to one-and-a-half centimeters.

We kept all cigarettes in the same place and usually one nonsmoker in the group was in charge of them, so they lasted longer and were distributed quite evenly. In the beginning, when we had enough cigarettes, we used to smoke one cigarette per hour, but later, when they became rare, one cigarette every three to four hours. Some camp inmates collected butts, using the remaining tobacco to make cigarettes with any sort of paper. The situation became much easier when family visits were allowed, and camp inmates received cigarettes or fresh tobacco with cigarette paper. One of the heaviest smokers was Radomir Glišić, who used to say that he wouldn't regret being killed if he were given as many cigarettes as he could smoke. Ratko Đukić, called Charlie (he got this nickname from Charlie Chaplin because of his characteristic walk), was trying to make cigarettes from dried chestnut leaves that he first washed, then dried, cut and rolled in paper, but whenever he lit it in the room such a smoke and stench was created that men had to leave the room promptly. The only case when cigarettes became disgusting for us was when our torturers were extinguishing them on different parts of our bodies. Whether it was because of the pain or something else, I don't know, but nobody was able to smoke then and only a dead silence was kept.

Sleeping

Sleeping without blankets and cushions was a great problem because we didn't have more than one square meter of space for each of us. In the night when trying to sleep, we were packed like sardines in a tin. We slept lying on our sides because there was not enough space to lie on our backs. If somebody had to get up and urinate, on his return he wouldn't find any empty space where he was lying before and would have to spend the rest of the night sitting or standing. Those were fortunate whose place was next to the wall, because they could lean on the wall, while those in the middle had to lean on somebody else and were not satisfied at all. During almost the whole night, one could hear mumbling and swearing because somebody was leaning on somebody else or pushing him, somebody's feet were smelling bad, and so on. During summer, the windows were open so we had enough fresh air, but when fall came and then winter, those sleeping under the windows were cold and those on the opposite side were lacking air, so we didn't know whether to close the windows or open them, and there was always somebody feeling dissatisfied.

It became easier for us when the first exchanges started, so those who remained in the room were pleased if somebody left the room for an exchange. There was now more space; you could now sleep normally lying down on a wooden floor. After the first visit of the International Red Cross (IRC), when visitors saw where we were sleeping, they brought us one blanket each and the conditions for sleeping improved considerably.

Ostoja Milanović in the Visoko War Camp, 1992-1993

Ostoja was also imprisoned in Germany from 1942-1945

*FC Napredak (a football club in the village Radovlje). They were all
in the camp except two of them.*

*Standing (from the left): Relja Milanović, Djordjo Milanović, Miloš
Milanović. Crouching: Luka Milanović, Zdravko Milanović*

Left: The girl in the middle is Višnja Bajić (daughter of Boban). Born June 24, 1982; killed June 20, 1992

Camp Visoko, photograph belonged to the JNA (photographed in the '60s)

Vaso "Vase" Mičanović, exchanged on July 7, 1992

Gordan Ćulum, wounded June 20, 1992 in his right leg

Novica Milanović, in prison from June 20, 1992, to April 4, 1994

Milorad "Šoja" Stojančević. Wounded September 25, 1992, when a grenade exploded in room No. 4

Luka and Zdravko Milanović: uncles who covered for Milenko while he wrote his diary

Trifko Glišić (third from left). Killed in prison camp, September 25, 1992

Work in the Camp

Prisoners enslaved in the Muslim camp at Visoko since June 20, 1992, were used as free manpower. They asked us to perform different kinds of work, work of general interest for the Muslim army but also for the private needs of guards and soldiers. The principal job was digging trenches on the frontlines. We had been digging almost the whole length of the frontline separating the Muslim from the Serbian army. When digging trenches in the area of the camp, nine prisoners were wounded; while on the battlefield Zbilje, two camp inmates digging trenches were wounded. By pure chance, nobody was killed. We worked hard—hungry and exhausted, naked to the waist even in the winter, under rain and snow. We were pushed to work like cattle. Before winter 1992, we were taken to cut wood for the needs of the Muslim army. They transported us to Gornja Zimća (a Serbian village in the direction of Kiseljak where Croatians lived), where we had to cut wood then load it by hand onto the trucks, tractors and animal-drawn vehicles. The forest where we were cutting wood belonged to old Serbian families Jovašević, Sprečo and Kretija, who had been living there for hundreds of years, and now they were expelled or killed. On one occasion, I also cut wood in the forest of a cousin of mine, Vlajko Jovašević, whose house and stable were burnt down and who was compelled to leave everything he possessed.

We were also working in the area of the village Gorani cutting the wood that belonged to Serbian families Samardžić, Kuvać and Čurić. The fundamental objective, besides material profit, was to rob, destroy and incinerate everything that was Serbian, so that no proof remained that those people ever lived there.

Profile of Camp Inmates

As is true of people everywhere, not all imprisoned Serbs were ideal, and there were strong differences between individuals. Serbs had been living in this region for hundreds of years as honest citizens who respected the law, and now, overnight, they were put behind bars—not because they were guilty under the law, but because they were considered guilty due to their national origin and Christian beliefs.

Taking into account that the men at Visoko had to adapt to hunger and thirst, fear of physical and psychic torture, the uncertainty of whether they would survive, and isolation from their families, one could say that in spite of all of this suffering, they behaved in an absolutely human and proud manner. You cannot help somebody more than you can help yourself, nor can you help anyone else before you help yourself. In those very difficult conditions, one tried first of all to help the wounded and sick men, older men, and children. In the beginning we had enough food and cigarettes, and, gathered into groups of ten to fifteen people, we distributed what little we had. We discussed our sorrow. Joy was rare.

When two meals were cut off, some of the men showed their true faces, thinking only of themselves, and we saw that we were mistaken in thinking of them as good neighbors. How to explain the fact that in those moments of hunger, S.S. left the baked chicken out to get spoiled, which we saw the day after in the garbage can? Or that R.G. let cheese that he was hiding from others turn green? How to explain that G.C. was stealing food from his nephew, whenever the latter went out to work? Considering the lack of food, even that behavior could be justified because each man had to think first of himself, then of others.

Of all the prisoners in the Visoko camp, only one camp

inmate showed an inhumane face. It was M.F., who was the only informer and spy for Asim Hamzić (the principal investigator and torturer). As the wife of M.F. was in "good relations" with Asim Hamzić, she often brought her husband food from home, while the others hadn't even bread. He also had some privileges with the guards. In return, M.F. was transmitting everything that men were doing or saying in the prison. He was the only spy among us. Before we discovered he was a spy, many of us, including myself, got beaten, not knowing why. I was chosen as the leader of our room, and during that time I didn't let him have any privileges over anyone else. Because of this he told Hamzić and Mrčo that I was making false insults and accusing them of using drugs and beating us, which were not true. After that I was called out and beaten.

Brothers Malešević discovered his treason after I was beaten, because M.F. told Hamzić that I had said that Muslims were taking drugs and then beating prisoners. He behaved in the room as if he was a chief; he took food without waiting his turn, while somebody else was not having any food. He drank water without waiting his turn, made cynical observations, and other behavior. If somebody had tried to oppose him after M.F.'s exit to the hall, he would be invoked to leave the room and was beaten. That is why we simply sat quiet if he approached our group and didn't say anything while he was with us. We knew everything, but we couldn't do anything. We sighed with relief when he was exchanged through International Red Cross on December 23, 1992, and taken to Montenegro, Yugoslavia. He lives and works now in the United States.

It was the only example of inhumane behavior from one Serb—if one could call him a Serb.

Tragicomic Situations

Although our lives in the camp were in danger at all times, and the fear of beatings could be felt in the air, we never lost our sense of humor. Rajko Milanović, nicknamed Rajcin, was undoubtedly the first to find the humor. He would make good natured jokes at everybody's expense, which made all of us laugh, after which the tension would ease and the room would be filled with the murmur of voices, talk and jokes. During the first days after his arrest, he said jokingly that not everyone left the camp alive. Unfortunately, this remark later came true. Here are some examples of the tragicomic situations in the camp.

On July 5, 1992, we cleaned the park and tilled the flowers, and after we finished the work, the guard let us pick some plums, *zerdelije,* which were growing there. Vaso "Vase" Mičanović, Stamenko Krsmanović, Dragan Živanović, Rajko Aksić and I were in the group. When we shared the plums in the room, Rajcin told me they were still green. Tomorrow the same group went to work and got beaten. When we came into the room all black and blue, there was silence. Everyone gathered around us and started putting wet poultices on us to ease our pain. When Rajcin saw my back all black and blue, he said, "It seems that the plums are ripe now." Eveybody started laughing, and we made jokes for a long time on that account.

Borislav Cvijetković, nicknamed Lav (Lav means Lion), who used to live next to the orthodox church in Visoko, was brought in and asked to surrender arms. They beat him up several times and you could not recognize his face because of the blood. The last time he was taken to Mrčo, Mrčo said to him, "You must find a rifle or I will kill you." Lav replied, "Mrčo, I have no rifle. Kill me, but leave it for tomorrow, for I am all broken up today." Mrčo laughed and said, "Go Lav, fuck your mother, when you are so crazy." After that he didn't beat him any more, and from then on, we used to say, "Leave it for tomorrow, skip it today," whenever something had to be done.

When we were trying to fall asleep on July 15, 1992, Šaćir Burko suddenly opened the door around 11:00 p.m. and asked into the dark, "Is there anyone from Dobrinja?" As no one answered, somebody asked if Buzić Mahala (the neighboring village) would do? Šaćir answered positively and Stevo Gavrić and Radovan Živanović went out. Some fifteen to twenty minutes later, they came back. As it was dark and we couldn't see anything, we only heard Stevo saying: "They have killed me, fuck their mothers." There was silence in the room, and they both took wet rags to ease the pain. When everything got quiet and the tension eased, someone from the corner of the room asked, "Will B. Mahala do?" Then someone from the other corner answered, "Yes, yes." After that, a muffled laugh was heard and we joked for a long time about the beatings these two got.

The Testimonies

BRANISLAV "BRANO" ĆEBO, son of MILAN
D. Zimća – Visoko
Now resides in Bjeljina, Serb Republic

At the beginning of the war in Sarajevo, the first clash that broke out between Visoko and Ilijaš was on May 3, 1992. Muslim forces then surrounded the mixed village of Kula Banjer, where they captured all the Serbs and brought them to the barracks in Visoko. They were in the barracks for four days and on the fifth they were exchanged with Ilijaš. The Serbs who returned and remained at their homes were taken to the barracks again after June 3, when the Muslim side started arresting all the other Serbs in localities around Visoko. I broke my leg on June 3, at 8:30 p.m., at Golo Brdo, where I was operating the radio station at the Donja Zimća company headquarters. Since Visoko was under Muslim control, we asked the Muslim authorities whether we could enter Visoko, so that my broken leg could be put into a cast. They said we could, so I, Bogdan Šavija, who was driving, and Radivoje Glišić, who accompanied us, went there.

They fixed my leg and instead of driving me home, three military policemen drove me to the Department of Internal

Affairs, saying that they would take me home tomorrow. When they brought me to the department I found a Serb from the town who was detained there; his name was Jovan Bilal and he was their worker. Half an hour later they brought Sveto Vujisić and twenty minutes after that Duško Nikolić, both from the city. Sveto Vujisić had already been beaten up when he was brought there, and he was beaten some more there in the corridor in front of the prison. Bogdan Šavija and Radivoje Glišić were returned from the health center before the curfew, i.e. before 10:00 p.m. The following day, on June 4, 1992, we were transferred, at about 1:00 p.m., from the Department of Internal Affairs to the barracks guarded by the Muslims, and then they started beating us because we had been brought in first.

They started blindfolding us, tying our arms and legs and beating us senseless. Later, they took my blindfold off, and I saw some of the denizens of Visoko who had beaten us. They were: Nedžad Graho, his brothers Dževad and Jasmin Graho, Samir (alias "Domac"), Adnan Babić, Amir Murtić, Miralem Čengić, Fejzic (alias "Daidža," I don't know his given name), Hajrudin Halilović (alias "Mrčo," brother of the commander Sefer Halilović), "Konzerva" (a merchant from Kakanj, I don't know his true name) and many other masked people. Not half an hour would go by without someone entering our room in the barracks and beating us.

On June 6, 1992, in the evening, they brought in Risto Cvijetić, while Sveto Vujisić died as a result of the beating during the day. On June 9, 1992, they brought Slaviša Božić and Ratko Popić; they brought Vaso Čurić, a reputable Serb from the town, about seventy-two years old; and Mihajlo Babić, a teacher of history from Visoko, about sixty-seven years old.

In a period of seventeen days, until June 20, 1992, about 137 Serbs were brought in from Gracanica, Podvisoko, Gorani, Selo Grad, Luka—a suburb of Visoko—Kula Banjer, Kralupi and Grajani.

During that period, somewhere around June 14 or 16, Slobodan Gogić also died as a result of beating and the Muslims later said that Sveto Vujisić had drunk cyanide and that Slobodan Gogić's heart had failed during the interrogation. We were also beaten by denizens of Bratunac who had been brought to Visoko.

I cannot think of a thing they did not use to beat us: Boots, helmets, rifle stocks, wires, round pipes, square pipes, nightsticks, ax handles, pickax handles, plastic grenade launchers, sand bags.

All this was done covertly. Serbs were brought in by night so that no one knew that the camp existed until June 20, when they brought in people from the villages of Paljike, Kalotići, Dobrinja, Poriječani, Mulići, Gunjace, Vilenjak, Pucisce and others. Until then, the first man in the camp was the commander of the territorial defense of Visoko—Kadir Jusić—who beat people himself and also had a team who beat and interrogated people for him.

The camp at Visoko was officially announced on June 20, 1992; Zijo Kadrić was appointed its warden and guard commanders and guards were also appointed.

The guard commanders were: Suljo Burko, a teacher; Šačir Burko, a worker from Kovina; Sead "Šicko" Kadrić, brother of the camp warden; and Besim Kulović, a house painter from Visoko. They themselves beat people and they also had people in shifts to beat us.

The only time when we were not beaten was from 11:00 p.m. to 6:00 a.m., and then the beatings would start every half hour. They also threw in cannon charges with fuses to hurt us and scare us, and HOS members—Muslims who had been in the Croatian war theatre and who had returned to Visoko wearing HOS uniforms and insignia—also wanted to slaughter us.

This is a brief account of the period from June 3, 1991, until the existence of the camp in Visoko was announced.

Branislav Ćebo

MLADEN MARIĆ, son of DRAGUTIN
Born on July 8, 1954 in Visoko, lived in the village of
Zbilje, 1.5 km from Visoko towards Kiseljak. Now resides in
Melbourne, Australia.

After the attack on Ilijaš from the direction of Visoko on
May 3, followed by some sort of a truce and calm period and
then a repeated attack on June 3, 1992, the Serb population
from Zbilje could not freely move or leave their houses. We
were totally surrounded by Muslim forces. They offered us the
option of joining the then Territorial Defense (TO—later the
B&H Army), which three or four Serbs accepted.

Sometime at the beginning of August, the entire Serb
population was officially put under house arrest in three larger
Serb houses (one of them mine), with guards around the clock.
At that time there was a Muslim brigade from Zenica in the
village, whose members started touring Serb houses, explaining
that they were searching for hidden weapons and material,
when their main job was to plunder foreign currency, technical
appliances, food, clothes and footwear.

Around September 10 to 15, they started taking us for
interrogations to their headquarters, housed in a summer
cottage in the village. It was all but interrogation. They beat
us for days, they broke our ribs and arms, and they shot our
neighbour Milutin Lukić. Ilija Kakuća, sixty-three years old,
was so beaten up that he could not stand for over three months,
and they would not allow him to seek medical attention.

Such maltreatment lasted until October 12, 1992, when eight
of us, in whose houses automatic rifles had been found, were
taken to what is known as the Isolation Camp of Visoko, where
we found numerous Serbs who had been captured, mainly in
June, in the villages around Visoko.

As for the "interrogations" in Zbilje, different methods and
tools were used. They beat us with electric cables, hammers,
clubs, rifle stocks, pickaxes, axe and shovel handles, and, of
course, with their feet, kicking us in the head, belly, kidneys.
They put bombs in our mouth, took us out to be "executed" and
brought us back, and as I already said, one of my neighbors was

executed.

When we came to the Visoko camp, we were taken to Asim Hamzić for interrogation again. In the corridor in front of Hamzić's office, Hajrudin "Mrčo" Halilović "worked on us" a little (he is claimed to be Sefer Halilović's brother), and promised that we would come to him for a "talk." Fortunately, thanks to some misunderstandings with the authorities of Visoko, Mrčo went somewhere and that we avoided that "talk."

In the Visoko camp we were taken to dig trenches near Serb positions every day, load timber for the Muslim soldiers and do other physical tasks. Two wounded men, Drago Vanovac and Siniša Vučenović, also had to dig trenches. We were taken to these works regardless of the weather and the situation in the war theatre.

According to these soldiers from Zenica, their brigade commander was Ibrahim Purić, called Tara, and the commander of the company that was in our village and carried out the so-called "investigations" was Amir Bečić. The most extreme and bloodthirsty among the soldiers was Ferid Šljivo.

On March 8, 1993, I was transferred, together with my neighbours from Zbilje, to the Zenica camp where our position was much better, except for the problems with food we had on several occasions. On three occasions we were not given any food at all: In the first case it lasted for three days, in the second for nine and in the third, twelve days without any food whatsoever, apart from that brought by our relatives during visits. I have to emphasize that the Orthodox priest from Zenica, Father Miroslav Drinčić, brought some food every Friday, which we, the inmates, shared and were thus saved from starvation for some time.

The happiest day was October 9, 1993, when, through the exchange with the Muslim side, we were transferred to our territory, to long-awaited freedom.

Mladen Marić

DEJAN MIČANOVIĆ, son of RATKO
Born on November 3, 1970 from Kalotići – Visoko
Now resides in Saint Petersburg, Florida

I was taken prisoner on June 20, 1992, in the village of Kalotići when the Muslim army attacked. The attack began at approximately 6:00 a.m.; in fact, I was awakened by the sound of the firing, which really surprised me. When I got dressed I went outside where I found Vladimir and Jovan. The firing was deafening and I was wounded in both arms during the attack, while my friend Vladimir was killed. My neighbours came to my assistance, administered first aid, and then another wounded man, Gojko Duvnjak, his son and I were to be taken to the medical centre in Visoko, but they took the three of us to the veterinary station in Moštre, where they maltreated and beat us.

We stayed there until 11:00 a.m. After that they took us out and threw us into a truck with the other prisoners and drove us to the camp at Visoko. They put us in an empty room and I found a place in a corner. Milenko D., Stamenko K., Vukan K., Milenko M., Bogdan, Saka M., Jovan M., etc. were there with me. Then Milenko, who had a bandage, dressed the wounds on my arms. About 7:30 the camp warden came in and asked if anyone was hurt, so I went out with Milenko M. since I was afraid to go alone. After that a doctor dressed my wounds and told me I had to go to the medical centre to have the bullet taken out of my arm since they would do that better there. If I had known what would happen I would have never gone. The warden called two police officers to take me to the medical centre. They took me and said that I had no need to be afraid and that everything would be all right. When we arrived, a large number of Territorial Defense members were in front of the medical centre building.

Then they began beating me until the doctor arrived and took me for x-raying. I was taken through a hall where their wounded were lying and they too hit and cursed me. When they brought me to the room where a man and a woman doctor were operating, the bullet was taken out of my arm and the wound bandaged. They told me I had to have a cast on my arm since it was broken. When they put the cast on my arm, they left me alone in the hall. Various people came and beat me, and after that the doctor approached and took me away in order to give me some medicine and told me that I should come every other day to have my wound dressed; however, I never did go, not even once, because I was afraid to. I could hardly wait to return to the room in which we were confined. I don't know what time it was when they dragged me into the room, but I sat down at once since there was no space to lie down. There were too many men in the room and I had nothing to lie down on, and that was the day my camp life began, which was in no way easy.

Day by day went by and each was worse than the previous one. I never left the room, not even to take a bath. Dressing the wound was out of the question, since there was nothing in the room to do it with. The food was awful and after eighteen days spent in camp, they ceased bringing two meals, so that we only had lunch, which was made up of a small piece of bread and a little stewed vegetables, which was unbearable for me since I had lost a great deal of blood, but my friends gave me part of their portions so I could have more to eat. I did not have to go to forced labour because I could not work and that was very fortunate for me. I had my first bath after two months and my wound was dressed by Milenko (Skot) for the first time after, I don't know, thirty to forty days. In the meantime, the wound on my right hand got infected and smelly because it was not dressed. I am an invalid now since I cannot spread out my fingers.

The days were full of torture, but somehow they passed. Then they began to move us from room to room; I was first in room 3, then room 2 and finally in room 7, from where I began going to forced labour, to the woods in Gornja Zimća. I came out of that room with the help of the Red Cross on Decemebr 12, 1991. I will never forget the days spent in the camp, since I could not imagine that in the twentieth century I could be hungry and without cigarettes and that my neighbours, Muslims, could hate and torture me so, only because I was Serb. I was released on December 20, 1992, and left for Montenegro.

Dejan Mičanović

VUKAN KUPREŠAK, son of BOGDAN
Born on October 19, 1958, Kalotići 14, Visoko
Now resides in Kozarska Dubica, BIH

I lived in Kalotići with my family, where I had built a house. I was employed in the social enterprise Zvezda in Visoko, branch office IGM D. Moštre.

I went into the transportation business in 1990, and in time bought two trucks. I have two sons, one twelve and the other six years of age. Just as all the other locals, I was a loyal citizen and fulfilled all my civic duties and obligations.

On June 20, 1992, at 6:40 a.m., the Territorial Defense Units

(TO) of the Republic of Bosnia and Herzegovina launched an attack on our village. Vladimir Milanović (son of Radovan) was killed on that occasion, while Dejan Mičanović was wounded in both arms and Gojko Duvnjak in the right shoulder. As I had a good house and three trucks (two belonging to me and one to my brother-in-law) parked in front of the house and was a truck operator, two soldiers asked me for money and literally turned the house upside down, beating me. They put a gun barrel into my mouth and to my forehead asking me if I wanted them to kill me. They put me against a wall, together with Djordje Vučenović and my mother-in-law, Jela Mičanović. Suddenly one of them said that they were taking us to a camp. When they brought us to the village of Bradve, they interrogated us again, and then their commander, called "Major," put a gun into my mouth, wanting to kill me. After much provocation and beatings I was transferred to the camp of Visoko, where there were 152 of us in a seventeen-by-seven meter room. The good was bad, and they did not give us any water to drink. It was all unbearable. Each day one of us was beaten up and the atmosphere was hard to endure. People would faint from hunger. We used a bucket in the room for urination, and some men did not go out to relieve themselves for as many as thirty days; Dragan Marković endured a whole fifty-six days. On July 8, 1992, I was taken out into the yard of the barracks, where they beat me and made me yell at the top of my voice, "Allah Uegber," almost all day long.

After that, my roommates teased me and put poultices on me. On July 2, 1992, Muslims entered our room disguised in HOS (Croat Defense Forces) uniforms (we knew them all personally) and took me and Željko Milanović (son of Veljko) out and beat us in front of everybody, while an ex-taxi driver from Visoko hit me on the head with a club.

Camp warden Zijad Kadrić made them stop, and all this was being done with the aim to scare and frighten us. Each day was the same—without food, water, salt—and constant beatings and provocations. The hardest day for me was August 3, 1992, when I had to dig trenches all morning and then, tired out, I returned to the room and sat down to rest. Then they called me out in the corridor. When I came out into the corridor, Mrčo was waiting for me there and took me downstairs to his room. He said that he needed a driver to move a truck and he and Zijo K. laughed. Fejzic, Murtić, Mrčo and two military policemen were in the room. They made me stand in front of the wall and beat me on the back with a club. When I fell on the floor they kicked me and beat me with nightsticks. Then they poured water over me and put me up against the wall again, continuing to beat me with a club and handles.

This lasted about half an hour (they told me this when I was carried back into the room). In the room I fainted and Boban and Milenko took me to the toilet, washed my face and put cold compresses on me. When I came to, I told Boban and Milenko that I would jump out of the window and kill myself if they beat me again. They comforted me and assured me that everything would pass and that we would all survive the camp. After that, to my good fortune, on August 12, 1992, I was transferred to the cellar prison, where they did not beat us. From there I was transferred to the Correctional Home in Zenica on November 5, 1992, where I was put on trial for service in the "Chetnik army" and sentenced to twenty-four months in prison. The treatment in Zenica was much better than in Visoko. We had beds, bathrooms and all the facilities that exist in real prisons, because this prison was over a hundred years old. The food was bad but we had much more freedom than in Visoko. Croat and Muslim deserters were also held there. The Red Cross paid more visits to the Croat prisoners than to us and brought them food. But we endured it all and I was exchanged on August 20, 1993, with the Mrdić family from Pale-Rakova Noga. When I left prison I weighed sixty-eight kilograms, and I had weighed 105 kilograms when I was arrested. For everything I went through, there is, in my opinion, only one reason—and that is that I am a SERB.

Vukan Kuprešak

JOVAN (JOCO) MILANOVIĆ, son of LUKA
(Now resides in Richmond, Virginia)

My name is Jovan Milanović. I was born on February 2, 1967, in Sarajevo. I lived in the town of Kalotići near Visoko. I was employed in the thermal power plant Kakanj in the commune of Kakanj in Čatići. I worked until June 15, 1992, when I was sent on temporary vacation because there was no work.

My town was one of a number of towns with a majority Serb population in the commune of Visoko. The commune of Visoko was quiet until May 3, when the Territorial Defense forces of B&H, i.e. Muslim units, attacked the territory of the commune of Ilijaš—the village of Kralupi with a mixed population and the village of Čekrčići with a Serb population.

Prior to these attacks and after that, life went on peacefully in our region. The villages: Topuzovo Polje, Biskupići, Muhašinovići, Donja Zimća, Gornja Zimća, Pučište, Novo Naselje and Bradve (with mixed populations), Kalotići, Maurovići II (Paljike), Vilenjak, part of Radovlje, Kondžilo, Dobrinje were in the commune of Visoko—in the direction of Kakanj, i.e. between the towns of Visoko and Kakanj—in the Sarajevo-Zenica valley to be more precise.

The Yugoslav People's Army, which was in the Ahmet Fetahagić barracks in Visoko, withdrew from them; I don't know the exact date, but I think in March. We, i.e., these Serb settlements, were partially armed, probably by the JNA, so that we organized night and day guards, everyone in his own settlement. During guard duty we toured the houses and their surroundings, up to specified spots. We were surrounded by "neighbouring" Muslim villages. As far back as I can remember, with the exception of minor incidents, there were no major problems in our joint life.

The Muslim villages were also armed and also organized guard duty like we did. During a period of time we even had joint guards. At the beginning there were no provocations, just an occasional bullet fired in the night, mostly from the Muslim side, but everything was peaceful. But the atmosphere was very tense. We lived, moved, but everything was not exactly all right. Both we and they knew we were armed and that the guard duty was organized. We started it in February 1992. I must mention that during this entire period there were constant negotiations between what are known as crisis headquarters, to prevent incidents. Then the first barricades were put up, in the village of Bradve, on the road to D. Moštre (a Muslim settlement). Our Muslim "neighbours" blocked the road with a truck.

That happened in March. We—Predrag Cvijetić, Duško Vuković and I—set out from D. Moštre in the morning, at 6:00 a.m.—and came to the barricade. "Neighbours," we asked, "what is this?" And Fuad Mušinbegović, Centrotrans driver, answered, "Because of your people from Ilijaš." We crossed the barricade and came to the place called Hanovi, where we saw many of our neighbours in arms. We stayed there a short while. No one bothered us, but it was not pleasant. We went back and informed the others, so that we too were ready. The days passed like that. Only the tension intensified. It was as if we were in some sort of an open camp, because we were surrounded by Muslim villages, and both sides had guards. You could not go anywhere in the evening, except to the territory of the villages of Kalotići, Maurovići II and Vilenjak, which were located in a triangle and linked. There were no Muslim villages between us and these three villages, while with all the other Serbian villages there were.

The villages were mixed in this way throughout central Bosnia, and it was not advisable to move farther from this zone, even during the day. As the months went by, the situation deteriorated, posing a great psychological burden on all of us. After an incident, tensions would grow, then things would calm down to normal and then—"Here we go again." What is funny in all this is that the crisis headquarters assured us that in the previous war there had been no trouble here so there wouldn't be any now—after all, we were "neighbours." This cost us the most. But the division was plain as day, because the Serbian population would not join the then Territorial Defense of B&H because it was a Muslim army.

A decision was brought in May to evacuate the population unfit for battle (old people, women, children) to Serb territory (Ilijaš) while the roads were still more or less open, because these Serb settlements had no direct borders with Serb territory. Thus, on May 13, a part of the population (mainly women and children, but not all of them, because you could not make anyone leave by force), left the villages of Kalotići, Maurovići II and Vilenjak (as well as from other villages) and went to Ilijaš. A larger number of them remained. The old people said, "I will not leave my house, even if I have to die." After that the roads between Visoko and Ilijaš were completely blocked.

The tension grew. Life in the village consisted only of guard duty, sleeping, all sorts of stories and waiting. TV and radio communications were not cut. In certain places the so-called reserve militia, consisting of Muslims, had its checkpoints. There weren't any particular provocations, except on the Muslim religious holiday of Bairam, when shooting started about five thirty in the morning and lasted all day, but only in the air, not on houses and elsewhere. What is strange in all this is that the crisis headquarters continued to negotiate on peace, joint life and non-provocations.

They even went so far as to form a mixed unit to guard these joint territories. Four or five days before the attack on our settlement, the villagers held a meeting with the command of the TO of Visoko, where it was said that there would be no problems or attacks. Pure trickery, in my opinion. Before that, in June or even in late May, I am not sure, some Serbs were taken to the barracks for interrogation. They were, among others, Branislav Ćebo, Jovan Bilal and Risto Cvijetić, whom I know. They stayed there. I learned that they were maltreated and beaten unconscious. Branislav Ćebo had a broken leg and was taken to the Health Center in Visoko to have it put in a cast, and from there Muslim soldiers took him to the barracks. We found him there when we were taken in.

Then came Friday, June 19, 1992. A day like all others. I was going to Paljike, i.e., Maurovići II, to see Slaviša Raković. I stayed a while at his place and returned home. About 2:00 p.m. Nenad Vanovac was arrested in D. Moštre and taken to the barracks in Visoko for interrogation. He spent several hours there, and was then released. Nenad says that he saw Brano Ćebo, Jovan Bilal, Risto Cvijetić and others there and that they were all beaten up. All our villages were alarmed. We wondered what would happen next. Guard duty was intensified during that night between Friday and Saturday, June 19-20. There were no signs that there would be an attack on Serb villages.

On Saturday at about 6:25 in the morning, random shooting on our houses started from all directions from the Muslim villages surrounding us. The attack started on the part of Kalotići bordering on the Muslim village of Hlapčevići. The battle lasted about three hours and ended with the surrender of weapons, mainly light ones. Vladimir Milanović (birth date 1971) was killed in that battle and the following were wounded: Dejan Mičanović (1970) in both arms, and Gojko Duvnjak (1932) in the shoulder. They gathered the others who were fit for battle near the house of Gojko Duvnjak, while the women, children and old people were gathered in the centre of the village. Before that they took Dejan Mičanović and Gojko Duvnjak away, purportedly to give them medical assistance. We learned later from them that on the way they had been beaten by rifle butts and barrels in the back, and that naturally, no medical assistance had been extended to them. They brought my father Luka Milanović (1936), Savo Milanović (1928), Veljko Milanović (1934) with their hands tied with wire behind their backs. With women and children crying, they led us away towards Moštre, where they detained us at Bradve (a Muslim village) to search us. There we were maltreated, beaten, provoked.

In the attack I recognized the following: Enver Begić (a neighbour from Bradve), Trako (I do not know his first name) from Ozrakovići near Visoko; Rušid from Liješeva; and Jasmin from Buci. I did not know the others. While we were at Bradve, they brought the women, children and old people, everyone who had remained in the village. They literally loaded them, like cattle, on a truck belonging to Vukan Kuprešak, which they had stolen, and drove them to a home in Hlapčevići where they spent seven days. During those seven days, while the village was empty, they plundered it. From Bradve they loaded us on a truck with a tarpaulin, which was driven by one Salem "Žućo" Zerdo; I used to know him well

He said that they were taking us to be exchanged. They brought us to the barracks in Visoko. There were many Muslim soldiers in front of the barracks. They did not beat us, but they cursed. Then they took us to the cellar, where we waited about an hour or two until Nezir Lopo and two other soldiers came to put us on the lists. The lists were made in alphabetical order, containing also the year of birth and father's name. The following persons from Kalotići were there: Savo Milanović, Veljko Milanović, Ostoja Milanović, Relja Milanović, Luka Milanović, Miloš Milanović, Radovan Milanović, Željko Milanović, Jovan Milanović (son of Luka), Jovan Milanović (son of Veljko), Gojko Duvnjak, Milenko Duvnjak, Vukan Kuprešak, Vaso Mičanović, Dejan Mičanović, Drago Cvijetić, Predrag Cvijetić, Slavko Masal and Siniša Vučenović, who is from Vilenjak and was in Kalotići during the attack. The cellar was very small; there were school desks in it, and it was very crowded and hot inside. The guards then went out and we were alone; we were not yet aware of where we were or what was happening, but reality itself reminded us of that. Blood from Dejan's arm was seeping on the tiles, because his wounds were dressed in a torn T-shirt. After one to two hours they brought people from Vilenjak and also made lists of them, and then they took us from the cellar upstairs to room No. 3. That was a dormitory in the barracks, and the impression was horrible, because everything in it had been demolished when the JNA pulled out. We started realizing that we had fallen into evil hands. The room was empty—like a hall—everything echoed. We all drew into one corner of the room. No one had anything because they had taken everything away. If we had at least a cigarette, we could chain-smoke it. The windows looked on Čekrčići—Serb territory, or more precisely Osijela, the first Serb lines, about 300-400 meters, or even less, from us.

Occasional shots are heard. It is hot, very stuffy. Radovan is with us. His son has been killed but he does not know that—his only son (1971). He also has two daughters. Who will tell him? He looks around, asking after him. I tell him—wounded, gone to hospital to Zenica. He just looks at me. I don't know if he believes me or not.

We are not afraid; we are not yet aware of what is happening or what will happen to us.

No one talks much. The door opens in the afternoon; before that the awful sounds of the lock, which will haunt me for the following three months in the camp in Visoko (probably the others, too).

After three months I was transferred to the Correctional Home in Zenica. Well-known faces of our neighbours and relatives from Maurovići II (Paljike) enter the room. No one speaks, we just look at each other. When they closed the door, we feel freer and come close to talk. We learn that they too surrendered after shelling and battle, because there was no way out. What is even worse, we learn that Igor Stojčić (1969) was killed by a shell, as well as Višnja Bajić (1980), that Dragan Cvijetić, called Branko, had killed himself with a spoon bomb. Blows, one after another, depression, sadness—we start realizing that things have gone to the devil . . . In the meantime, some other people from the surrounding Serb hamlets are brought in. Among them is Nedjo Ristić, nicknamed Saka, who was on the night shift when they captured him at work. He does not know that that morning they killed his son Željko Ristić (1966) and wife. He asks everyone about his son. Who can tell him? They were killed by Nisat Ramić from Seoća (a Muslim village in the direction of Kakanj). They shot the Damjanović family: Zoran Damjanović, his father and mother. Zoran, with seven wounds, remained alive, and was taken to a hospital in Zenica, later to the Correctional Home. He is now in Banja Luka.

We learned that in the village of Kološići (majority Muslim population), where the family Vuković lived, six members of that family were killed, shot: Boško Vuković, Draginja Vuković, Rajko Vuković, Milenko Vuković, Jelenko Vuković, Cico Vuković.

That is a story unto itself. It must be dealt with in detail. There are living witnesses who saw all that!

New Serbs were constantly brought in on June 20, 21 and 22. We were in five rooms on the upper floor. Some Serb women were there also. Of them I knew Ljuba Kuvać from T. Polje. There were about twenty-four of them, as far as I know, in the room across, room No. 2. There were 154 of us in room No. 3, where I was. I don't know how large it was, but I know that we were like sardines when we lay down. Mostly people from Paljike, Kalotići, Vilenjak, Porječani were in that room. They made new lists by rooms.

The first night. We lie down on the floor. A coat comes in handy, whoever has one. Whoever doesn't lies down on the bare floor. Boots or shoes under your head. Crowded, you cannot turn over.

Earlier they threw a bucket, about five liters, in the corner, behind the door. We ask, "What is that?" The guard says, "To urinate in. Don't anyone dare knock on the door." Madhouse. Those who can, sleep. During the night someone gets up to urinate, steps on your arm, your leg—let him step on your head too, fuck it.

In the morning, calluses on my ankle, hip and right shoulder. Next night, I sleep on the other side, and then there are calluses on that side too. You cannot lie on your back. But these calluses grow hard, you get used to it.

After that they threw in some overcoats, but not enough to go around. Grabbing. Quarreling. But better to share one than nothing.

In the beginning we got three meals, with a lot of salt, but not enough water. We had a soldier's water bag. It was drunk up quicker than you can say "čakija," as the Bosnians would say. And no one dared to ask if he could get some, because he'd be in for a celestial beating. We ate from old tin mess kits and lids, without spoons. There were six men to a mess kit and three to a lid. We made up groups at once. The mess kits were washed only once, and then nothing. We ate one after another, from mouth to mouth; it was hot, but you have to eat, because if you miss your turn once, perhaps it won't come again. After that, cold water! Most of us lost our teeth because of that. We got those three meals for about twenty days, and then we were told that they were cutting our breakfast and dinner. Without any explanation. Our troubles started then. We got a piece of bread each. Rich was the one who got the crust, even if he had only a mouthful more. This one meal was issued about 2:00 p.m. and then nothing until tomorrow at 2:00 p.m. (except beatings).

The saddest thing in this was that grandfathers, fathers, sons, grandsons were here together watching and enduring it all. Father gives me his share, and I give him mine, because I think he is older and will not be able to survive, and he gives me his because I am younger, I need strength because they beat me. And it is like this every day.

We go out to clean the yard and find pieces of bread, dry and hard like a rock, but as sweet as honey. When grandfather used to tell me what hunger was I did not believe him. I even laughed a little, but now I know and would wish it on no one. You feel your body being slowly exhausted, you feel it inside and outside, you feel every gram you lose. I did not believe that, and God forbid that I ever have to feel it again. It is strange that you feel it on yourself, and don't see it on others, and others don't see it on you, probably because we were all together all the time and could not notice that. We would notice when someone suddenly stood up, started shaking and fainted. Probably because of rapid loss of weight.

You stand up, you hear humming in your head, you start shaking and then fall to the floor. We encouraged and helped one another and what made it easier, if I can say so, is that most of us knew one another. Also, we were not aware of the situation, until the first beatings and interrogations.

We could go to the toilet and to wash our faces in the morning. They open the door. One hundred fifty-four of us—for fifteen minutes on the ground floor. You hardly get downstairs, your turn comes (there were two stalls), and then you "march" back again. No time to go to the toilet, let alone wash up—you can only dream of that. On the way back, in the corridor, they kick you in the back, hit you with pickaxe handles and things. It's potluck; sometimes you fare better, sometimes worse. Young people fare better—their backs are strong. The elderly—poorly. Then we use the bucket in the room as a toilet, and the heat drives you crazy. The bucket with urine spilled on the floor several times; that was awful. Lucky were those who could go relieve themselves. When we had just arrived and had three meals a day it was difficult, because you needed to use the toilet more often, then we had a madhouse for some twenty days. When we got one meal a day it was easier; you had to defecate less often, and it was not so crowded. For instance, you'd defecate every seven to fifteen days, and some people did not defecate for thirty-six, forty days, and Dragan Marković not for fifty-four days.

The beatings started on the third day. First Miloš Milanović was taken out and came back all beaten up, black as a mulberry, as the saying goes. For no reason whatsoever. He was born in 1934, a professor, accused of being a sniper, and almost totally blind.

Vukan Kuprešak, Predrag Cvijetić, Jovan Milanović (son of Veljko) were first taken for interrogation. They were not beaten. They were interrogated by the investigating magistrate Asim Hamzić. Various people entered the room to see the "Chetniks." Thus, a girl came. She entered the room dressed in uniform (we called her "Nura"), greeted them with "Akšam hajrula, Chetniks. Those of you Chetniks, fuck your mothers!" Several of them responded with "Allah ala rasola," probably for fear, and she started beating those seated closest to her with a rubber club on the heads. At the beginning we sat until HOS members—four of them—came in. "Stand up, fuck your Chetnik mothers, how many eyes did you gouge out and how many children's fingers did you cut off?" shouted one of them. The room was small, but we stood three lines all around it, so that a folk dance could have been danced in the middle. Knives in their belts, they walked around and looked everyone in the eyes, Asim Hamzić and Zijad Kadrić with them. Two young men fainted—Željko Milanović and Zoran Topalović.

They took Vukan Kuprešak and Željko Milanović and maltreated them in front of us. Then we realized the gravity of the situation. They beat us in different ways. Hajrudin Halilović, called Mrčo, came and took the first group to dig trenches around the barracks, forty people. Through the window we saw him kicking Milorad Stojančević, called Šoja, in the head, and him falling down. After that he came to the room laughing, he needed a second group of forty people. He picked forty people; I was among them. He was laughing all the time, but it seemed suspicious to me. When we went down, there were four guards waiting for us in front of the building. They lined us up in two lines and led us towards the edge of the yard where the previous group dug. They started shooting in the air and singing, "The Black Legion Goes to Battle." They said to us: "Heads down, don't raise your eyes." Nothing good to be expected. A sunny day, hot, July. Among the guards, I recognized Hasan Čizmić from Hlapčevići; we used to play football in the same club for a time. He seemed not to recognize me.

We dug trenches around the entire barracks, i.e., the barracks yard, which was really big. When they brought us, they lined us up so as to group us. I saw at once that there was trouble in store because the group that had dug before us, forty people, were exhausted, dirty, beaten up and did not dare look at us at all. And most of us knew one another very well. I saw the guards with wooden clubs. These were pickax handles.

We held pieces of bread in our hands because we had been told that we would get lunch there, where we were digging. We got "lunch," but across our backs—double portions of that! Bogdan Šavija, called Bodo, from D. Zimća, who was an inmate like us, was in charge of making a timetable of digging, and supervising and overseeing the work. Bodo was selected by Mrčo because he was a building technician by vocation.

They deployed us along a canal that was about a hundred meters long, half of which had already been dug by the first group, and we were to finish it. There were pickaxes, shovels, hoes already in the canal. Relja Milanović, Slaviša Vanovac, Uroš Vanovac, Zoran Damjanović, Aksić (I don't know his given name) and I were separated to an outlying trench about twelve meters long, about forty meters away from the others. The digging could start. To the screaming and singing of the guards we had to dig, but we were not allowed to raise our heads nor look around us. We had to dig with all our strength despite the fact that we were exhausted. Guards with wooden clubs walked along the trench, hitting everyone on the back, kidneys, spine. You did not dare turn around nor raise your head. It was sickening to hear the hollow, dull thud of the wooden club on one's back, but you did not feel fear, nor too much pain when it hit you. It was something that everyone got and that you had coming, too. Thus, they walked up and down the trench.

All this was accompanied by curses, insults, etc. Beside the trench there was an avenue of horse chestnuts, with a large crown, under which Mrčo, Fejzic, nicknamed Daidža, and two other guards—I don't know their names—were sitting in the shade and taking us out, one by one, under the crown of the chestnut and beating us there. They beat us savagely, taking away everything we had on us (gold, watches, money). Screams and moans and hollow blows were heard under the branches of the chestnut. We could not lift our heads to see, because we would then have to pay even more dearly. It was hot and the water from the hydrant was industrial water and they brought very small quantities of it. When we finished the trench, they lined us up in two rows and whoever did not have calluses on his hands got an additional beating.

They took us back to the room, which was very stuffy and filled with an unpleasant stench of urine and sweat, hurting the eyes like sulfur. But it was all right. Another day passes; one somehow survives. The others gathered around us immediately, making compresses from the linings of the overcoats, soaking the rags in water—we had little water, but we had to do that, our backs and kidneys were more important. We started being more and more afraid of them. We were becoming aware that playing had ended and this was cruel reality. The digging continued during the next days, but with fewer beatings.

In any case, in addition to the canal, every exit from the room to do something was, as a rule, accompanied by a beating.

The room represented some sort of security—not much, but still, security.

The beginning of the inquiry and interrogation by the real "investigators" is a story in itself. It was allegedly a regular investigation. Statements were made, and they looked them over, making a selection of who would undergo investigation proceedings and who wouldn't. During those interrogations there was no beating or maltreatment (at least not in my case, nor I think in the case of all the others). The investigators were Nurija, Ivica, Burge (Burgijašević) and some others, I don't know their last names.

The investigation conducted by Asim Hamzić and Mrčo was much harder and bloodier. They took people individually to their room, a floor lower (the so-called "shock treatment" room) and conducted their investigation there. The room was approximately six by four meters, with shades on the windows. Lockers were placed in front of the windows, probably because of the sniper shooting at the barracks from Osijela.

Entering the room itself was awful, because the walls were dirty, smeared with blood, and different instruments, such as wooden clubs of different sizes, wooden sticks, rubber sticks, rubber hoses, boxes, etc. were strewn around in the corners. Mrčo's group, which consisted of four, sometimes five or six people, beat and interrogated people in that room. Amir Murtić, Fejzic (Daidža), Miralem Čengić, Esnaf "Esno" Pulić and Samir "Domac" Selimović were in that group.

Sometimes, they would dress in black ninja suits and put you with your arms in the air and your face on the wall and beat you with whatever they got hold of, wherever they could. It was awful that the screams from that room were heard in all the rooms in the camp, and that the fathers could hear the screams and moans of their sons.

The first packages with food were brought by Ivica Stojčić, a Croat who lived in our village because he was married to a Serb woman—Dušanka Topalović. Their son Igor (1969) was killed during the attack on June 20, 1992. He helped a lot the women and old people who had remained in the villages after we were taken away. Now Ivica Stojčić is in the Correctional Home in Zenica accused of having killed a Muslim soldier. Those packages with food were first inspected by the guards, who took everything they liked and threw a bit to us in the rooms. They took cigarettes, meat, cookies, etc.

The first visits that they allowed brought immeasurable joy and sadness. The women who had brought food had to take it out and put it on a table and we could eat only there; they would not let us take it to the rooms. A sad sight to behold, mountains of food; we devoured everything like animals, because we had only five minutes. We ate meat and pie, tomatoes, apples, cookies, coffee, milk, all at the same time. The women watched us and cried. We were thin, sad, exhausted.

I spoke barely two words to my mother during that first visit. "How are you, son?"—"I am fine." She cried, and I ate like crazy. Then the visit was over, finished—good-bye. And they took us to the rooms. Those in the room expected some food, but there was nothing. Sadness. I managed to hide some bread and some pie in my belt, and two apples in my trousers' pockets.

After that they allowed us to bring food to the rooms. The first visit of the International Red Cross took place on August 6, 1992—they came to register us. In the beginning no one believed that it was the International Red Cross. We did not dare take their forms and fill them in. Later, we talked about everything (when we had assured ourselves that they really were the International Red Cross). They gave us two packs of Opatija cigarettes each and some soap for washing clothes. After they left, things became worse because we had complained of the food—naively!

We bathed for the first time after thirty-six days. Without soap, a change of underwear, towels. Three groups of fifty people each, fifteen showers, you just got wet, like a mouse. I washed my hands with soap for the first time in forty-two days or so.

Shells regularly fell into the barracks yard (because of Muslim mortars fired in front of the building itself and from the yard), from our positions in Ljubnići, I think, but none hit the building itself while I was there—until September 23, when I was transferred to the Correctional Home in Zenica. Shrapnel and bullets flew into the rooms. At the beginning we used to lie down on the floor with our arms over our heads, because the entire building was shaking.

Later, we would walk around the room as if nothing was happening, a matter of habit I suppose, and I would not regret being hit. We sometimes prayed to God that it hit us and let happen what will.

On July 17, 1992, they take fifteen of us outside to dig trenches in the yard, in the direction of Osijela on the very edge of the yard. The guards take us out, lead us to the place where we should dig and leave us. We start digging trenches others have already begun a day earlier. Then shells start flying over us, making a whizzing sound, towards Kula Banjer, above Visoko. We stop digging and take shelter as a guard who appears from somewhere orders. In the meantime, two guards try out a training grenade launcher beside us and give us a pack of Kolumbo cigarettes.

After that, everything becomes quiet and strangely calm. As soon as we have resumed digging I feel a strong detonation to my right, which throws me out of the trench; I hear nothing, shake my head, silence. All of a sudden I hear wails and cries. Čorba and Djidja are beside me—they too were thrown out of the trench. I am aware—a grenade. I look at myself. I am not wounded, but farther in the trench Saša, Željo, Zane, Milenko, Stojko, Daco and Njonja are lying; somewhat farther are Dule, Mane and Mirko—wounded. Djidja, Čorba and Branko have remained behind them. I look around, blood everywhere, I cannot believe my eyes. We carry them out of the trench to the guard post outside, across the barracks yard. They call an ambulance at once, and it arrived in about twenty to thirty minutes, I don't know exactly. They drive the wounded to the Health Center in Visoko. We remain, they take us back to the barracks. In the room, my uncle asks me about Saša, my cousin. I don't know what to tell him, I am not sure he will survive.

My trousers are spattered with blood, which only makes him more suspicious. But, thank God, he is alive, he is in Prnjavor now. Saša, Njonja and Zane were more seriously wounded and were at once transferred to the hospital in Zenica; after that, to the camp in the correctional home there. The other wounded were returned to the barracks and had somewhat better treatment than the others. I think that the Muslims fired the grenade on us—surely. Jovan Milanović, Manojlo "Mane" Vanovac, Mirko Kuvać, Branko Janjušić, Boban "Čorba" Vojnović and I were digging the trench—we were not wounded. Saša Milanović, Zane Radulović, Sladjan Šljivić, Željko Šljivić, Duško Raković, Jovo Krsmanović, Stojko Krsmanović, Davor Glišić and Milenko Despotović were wounded.

After that we went to mow hay in the yard. We mowed for the guards, we got some food. We mowed for several days and had to stop because of the snipers.

On August 25 I was taken to the Communal Court in Visoko where I, Mladen Milanović and Djordjo Bajić were sentenced by judge Sabina Buljušmić to thirty days of prison pursuant to Article 119, paragraph 2, item 1 on charges of service in the enemy army.

We were transferred from the camp premises to the cellar, i.e., prison, which we ourselves had built there. Some people, i.e., our friends, inmates, had already been taken down there. There were four rooms approximately four by four meters there. There was also a larger room there and it was partitioned with wooden panels. It contained two so-called "palaces" made of boards, a little space for walking, approximately four by one-and-a-half meters, and a slop pail in the corner. In some there was one and in some two windows, forty by sixty centimeters, with thick bars and no glass. We spent most of the time lying down (although we were not allowed to do that) because it was crowded and we could not walk. At one time, there were fourteen of us in each of those rooms. We got three good meals, we had other guards, something like civilian ones, they wore blue uniforms. At 6:00 in the morning, we went to the toilet and to wash up. After that we could only use the pail. Downstairs, we had spoons and everyone had his own mess kit. We were not especially maltreated, except for a few blows, slaps in the face and provocations.

The other two rooms in the cellar were adapted because more and more people were put into prison. On September 23, 1992, Djordjo Milanović, Siniša Milanović, Željko Milanović,

Novica Milanović, Mladen Milanović, Milovan Raković, Uroš Vanovac, Zoran Damjanović, Djordjo Bajić and I were taken to the Zenica Correctional Home in Zenica.

At the war-prisoner camp Visoko there were the following government officials:

Kadir Jusić – first camp warden
Zijad Kadrić – second camp warden

Shift leaders:
Suljo Burko
Šačir Burko
Besim Kulović
Sead Kadrić, nicknamed Šicko

Main investigators:
Asim Hamzić – chief inspector
Hajrudin Halilović, nicknamed Mrčo
Amir Murtić
Miralem Čengić
Fejzic, nicknamed Daidža
Elmedin Ahmić
Jasmin Pinjić
Esnaf Pulić, nicknamed Esno
Samir Selimović, nicknamed Domac
Namik Dizdar
Nisat Ramić—Committed the largest number of crimes in the region of Visoko. He was detained in the correctional home in Zenica. He slaughtered the father of Mike Ćulum, a policeman from D. Zimća.

Jovan Milanović

BOGDAN TOKIĆ, son of SLOBODAN
Born on January 26, 1966 in Visoko
(Now resides in Melbourne, Australia)

I lived in Visoko with my parents in our house at 15 a, Kalotići street. I worked in Energoinvest in Sarajevo as a qualified locksmith. I often travelled from Sarajevo to Visoko and I would sometimes spend the night in a rented flat in Sarajevo. When barricades were put up in Sarajevo I could no longer travel and I remained in Visoko. Serbs accounted for seventeen percent, Muslims for eighty percent, and Croats for three percent of the population of Visoko. The Stranka demokratske akcije—SDA (Party of Democratic Action) won at the elections in Visoko. Relations with our neighbours became tense.

I lived in the Serb settlement of Kalotići, about seven kilometers from Visoko. Kalotići was attacked on June 20, 1992 by Muslims from Zenica, among whom were many people from Sandzak who had mainly come after the war broke out. In our settlement we organized ourselves and had guard duty. We had automatic weapons from the former JNA. The army, i.e., the JNA, had left Visoko in April 1992 and gone to Pale. After being attacked we defended ourselves, but did not succeed because there were 2,500 of them and 150 of us. A lot of Serbs had fled Visoko in April and May so that a very small number had remained. There were many women, children and old people.

About twenty of our fighters were killed during the attack. Of them I know Vlatko Milanović, Dragan Cvijetić and Igor

Stojčić. I do not know the others.

They barged into Kalotići and arrested all of us defending the settlements. They also arrested the women, children and old people and took them to Donje Moštre, near Visoko to the Cultural Center and held them there for ten days. They took us combatants to a camp (the former Ahmet Fetahagić barracks). Four hundred fifty of us were taken away. They plundered our houses and after that let the women, children and elderly return home. In the camp, they beat and maltreated us. They accused us of being Chetniks. They beat us with iron bars, clubs, wooden sticks, rifle butts. There were 154 of us in the room, which was about 120 square meters. We slept on the floor. In fact, you could not lie down, but could only sit because there was no space. They took us out one by one from the room, and down to the cellar where they beat us. They forced us to confess where the weapons were. They beat us at all times, be it day or night. We were beaten by the brother of Sefer Halilović (former commander of the Muslim army, from Sandžak), I don't know his name, and an inspector from Visoko, Asim Hamzić.

They took us to the barracks yard to dig trenches and would beat us then. Vojno Raković, Trifko Glišić, I cannot remember the other names, but seven to eight people succumbed to the beatings in the camp. We had no toilet—nor a doctor. We relieved ourselves in a pail near the door, 154 of us used that pail. Two months after we were arrested, the International Red Cross came and registered us. The inmates who died, died before the arrival of the Red Cross, and no one died after that, but the situation deteriorated. The "green berets" were not present during our talks with the Red Cross, but the interpreter was a Muslim. After the Red Cross left, we were beaten even more. They asked us, "What did you talk about?" When the Red Cross came for a second visit, they forbade us to talk to them. We had to say that we were all right.

The food was extremely bad. Once a day, at 2:00 p.m., we would get a piece of bread with some sort of soup. Just like swill. We could not stand up for hunger, but could only sit and had to dig trenches in that condition, hungry and with beatings. The Primary Court in Visoko raised criminal charges two months after our detention for service in the enemy army and we were sentenced to a month of prison in the cellar in the barracks where cells had been built in the meantime. I spent a month there. Five or six of us were in that cell. Slobodan Tokić, Ranko Manojlović, Novica Kisić, Boban Vojnović and Uroš Vanovac were in the cell with me. After that we were all transferred from Visoko to Zenica, to the Correctional Home, room No. 1, where Šešelj Vojislav was once imprisoned. No one maltreated me in Zenica. They were very correct; they were mainly personnel who were previously employed in the Correctional Home.

They even talked to us. They talked about the time when Šešelj was serving his sentence there. There were sixty of us in room No. 1. We slept in bunks and had bed linen (and a toilet and two meals each day, at 9:30 a.m. and 4:00 p.m.). The food was bad, but much better than in Visoko. We had a TV set in the room. They would turn it on and turn it off at a specified time. We had a loud speaker in the hall so that we could listen to the radio. They also turned it off when it was time to go to bed. On Fridays and Saturdays we were allowed to watch TV until 11:00 p.m. Sometimes they let us watch video cassettes all day, when there were film marathons. Only volunteers who had signed a paper to that effect went to work and they were entitled to a third meal. On Monday and Friday we could see a doctor. I was allowed to have a lawyer during the trial in the District Military Court. The judge was a Serb, Mladen Veseljak. I was sentenced to two and a half years with the right of appeal. The lawyer, Vujadin Ivanović (a Serb), came to visit me twice a week. He was willing to defend people who did not have money to pay him.

I lodged an appeal, but it has not been yet reviewed because that is to be done by the Supreme Court—which does not exist. We were also visited by a priest—Miroslav Drinčić. He came every Friday.

I was exchanged on October 9, 1993, in the village of Ljubin Han, near Turbe, commune of Travnik. One hundred fifty of us, and I don't know how many of them were exchanged.

I came to Serbia on November 1, 1993. Before that I was in Bijeljina. On October 1, 1993, my friends in Požarevac took me in.

Bogdan Tokić
December 16, 1993

SLAVIŠA RAKOVIĆ
Born on January 27, 1966 in Visoko
(Now resides in Bratunac, Serb Republic)

I lived in Visoko (village of Maurovići) in a family house with my parents, brother and sister. I was employed in a private restaurant as a waiter. Visoko was predominantly populated by Muslims—80%. After the pre-election campaign, intolerance developed between the Serbs and the Muslims. There were provocations and insults addressed to Serbs in the coffee shop in which I worked. My boss was a Muslim, and I had no problems with him. Young people were the worst fanatics. I could no longer stand that pressure and voluntarily went to the Ahmet Fetahagić barracks. That was in February, 1992. When the Army left Visoko, I returned home. In March, TO and the Green Berets put up barricades around the Serb villages and at the entrance to the city.

Donja and Gornja Zimća and Maurovići are Serb villages. The villagers of Zimća managed to get out over Kiseljak (Croatian territory), and we were left in the middle. The Army retreated from Visoko in May. After that, on June 20, 1992, there was a Muslim attack on our village. We had some arms that the Army had left behind. We couldn't defend ourselves. They shelled us. This shelling killed Višnja Bajić, Igor Stojčić, Vlatko Milanović and Dragan Cvijetić. After that shelling they entered the village and called us by loudspeaker to gather. We surrendered, after which a search of the houses started. They put a hundred of us men on a truck and took us to the Ahmet Fetahagić barracks in Visoko. The women and children were taken to Hlapčevići (a village) to the communal office. They kept them there for seven days and let them return to their plundered homes.

The moment we were brought to the camp they started beating us. They beat us for three months on end, until the International Red Cross came and registered us. They took us to dig trenches. The beatings eased up somewhat after the registration by the Red Cross but still continued. The food was bad, one meal a day, consisting of rice cooked in water, while fifteen of us prisoners shared one loaf of bread. We slept on the floor. Some were wounded during trench digging. I remember that those were Sladjan Šljivić, Saša Milanović. They were seriously wounded and taken to Zenica hospital, and from the hospital to the camp in the correctional home. Once a grenade fell into our room. Trifko Glišić and Milo Krunić were killed on that occasion. There were many wounded. During that time I was in the cellar.

I was taken a few days before the shelling from that room to the communal court in Visoko where I was tried and sentenced to one month of detention. I was charged with service in the enemy army. I had no right to counsel. I cannot remember the name of the judge.

There were 160 of us in one room in the barracks. There were five hundred of us in the whole barracks. There were people from Visoko, but also from the surrounding villages. Twenty girls and women were also there. I don't know whether they were raped. They spent about thirty days in the camp. After the trial I was sentenced to a month in detention and taken to a cell in the cellar, where there were five of us. Jovo Milanović, Slaven

Stojančević, Siniša Topalović and Duško Raković were with me in the cell. The Muslims who maltreated us and whom I know and was even on good terms with once were Miralem Čengić, Amir Murtić, Hajrudin Halilović (brother of Sefer Halilović who was a commander in the B&H Army). The three of them were in charge of the beatings. They used to take two or three of us to the cellar to beat us, then would take us back to the room and take the next three, and so on.

During detention (in the cell) they did not beat us. After the detention they took us to the Correctional Home in Zenica. I was taken to Zenica for the main trial. I was accommodated in Pavilion No. 1, room No. 3. There were sixty of us in the room. We had beds and bed linen.

The food was also bad. On one occasion we didn't get food for ten whole days. An Orthodox priest came once every fortnight to see us. He would bring some food and cigarettes. There we had a TV set in the room. They used to let us watch films during film marathons. We had to abide by the house rules, which meant getting up at 7:00 a.m. and going to bed at 10:00 p.m. Work was not obligatory, but only those who wanted would go. From there we were taken to trial. I was sentenced to two years of prison for service in the enemy army, as per Article 199 of the SFRY Law. I had the right to a lawyer, but couldn't pay one. The court appointed one to defend me. The judge was Vlado Adamović, a Croat. He sentenced me to two years. However, I was exchanged on October 9, 1993, in Turbe. About 155 of our men were exchanged for 220 of theirs.

I arrived at Belgrade on December 23, 1993. Before that I asked to be in Bijeljina, Illijaš, Vogošća or somewhere else on free Serb territory. But there was place nowhere.

My father is still in the camp, my mother in Visoko, my sister in Bijeljina, and my brother was killed on the front in Trnovo.

Slaviša Raković
December 24, 1993

MILORAD JOVIČIĆ, son of STANOJE
(Now resides in Minneapolis, MN)

I was taken to the camp on August 7, 1992.

I spent some time in the camp of Visoko, and prior to that was two months in house detention, obliged to report every day. I was a member of SDS and participated in the organization of the party. When Visoko was shelled, there were twenty Serbs left in my settlement, who were cut off and could not break through the Muslim part so as to get out. I emphasize that they had managed to take their families—wives and children—out before that. Only a few people remained with us as they could not go on account of their age or illness. The cleansing of the village started and ten thousand fighters from Zenica came against us—fifteen hundred of us at most in all the villages. During the cleansing they started with the killings, so that we fled before them towards Kiseljak, which was held by the Croats. Most of the men remained behind to protect the women and children. During the retreat I was in the back lines. A lot of people were killed then, and even a whole family was shot at the threshold of their house.

My own best man was a Muslim who saved me from being killed or put in a camp. I was only held in house detention. As I already said, I reported daily and once two members of the Muslim army without any provocation put me into a car and took me to the Visoko camp. That is when the interrogations started, with daily physical torture. I was beaten up almost every day. They hit me with what was at hand, forcing me to confess to things I didn't know. The food was terrible and consisted of a slice of bread. I was of poor health and started urinating blood because of the hard blows I received and my infirmity.

I lost thirty-five kilograms, and many of my friends succumbed to the beatings and injuries. Those were twelve men and a woman, and they killed one of them by throwing him out of the window. On September 25, 1992, a grenade was thrown into the prison and luckily hit the window sill. On that occasion two men were killed and twenty-six wounded—some more and some less seriously. I was also wounded then, in my left leg, and had tiny shrapnel all over my body. That was the first time we received first aid in the camp. On average there were fifty of us in one room, four by five meters. This attempted massacre of theirs was to have been attributed to the Chetniks, i.e., the Serbs, just before the holding of the Summit Conferences in London and Geneva.

After this, journalists came, insisting that we give statements to the effect that Chetniks had attacked us. Naturally, we didn't want to say that, as it would be a stark lie and propaganda. After that they tried to kill us all by leaving the doors open so that their prisoners (deserters from their army) who were also in the cellar in another room could come in. On that occasion we were saved by one of their members, a former friend of a pal of ours. After about ten days we were visited by the Red Cross from Geneva, with a team of doctors, and they insisted that the living conditions in the camp be improved. The food became better then, we were allowed medical help and visits. After that I remained there the whole winter and on February 16, 1993, I was transferred to the prison in Zenica. Some of the people had already been exchanged in a local exchange, and about forty of us came to Zenica.

We were not maltreated in Zenica in this way, and the food was better. We even got two meals a day. We even got beds, and the rooms were heated a little. That meant much to us, exhausted as we were. There they raised charges and tried us. I was among them.

I was charged with possession of arms and sentenced to another nine months of prison. I remained there until April 28, 1993, when I was exchanged in the area of Teslić. This happened by pure chance. The Serbian army had a list of the people it wanted, and since some of them were missing I was included. At the court I had the right to a lawyer, who was a Croat and who helped me a lot during the pronouncement of the sentence and later when the exchange occurred. That is how I managed to get the mildest prison sentence.

Milorad Jovičić
July 22, 1993

TOMKA VUJISIĆ
Wife of murdered SVETOMIR VUJISIĆ

Biographical data of husband: Svetomir "Sveto" Vujisić, son of Boriša Vujisić, born on the 15th of March 1947 at Kolašin, Montenegro, murdered on the 6th of June 1992.

He came to Visoko in 1966 and found employment as a shopkeeper's assistant. Later he continued his education and graduated from the school of economics. Immediately before the war broke out, he was employed as an economist at Agro-coop Enterprise. In 1974 he married a girl from Čekrčići and that fact was fateful for him. He was arrested because he was from Montenegro and because his wife was from Čekrčići. He was arrested on the 4th of June 1992 and murdered immediately after interrogation and investigation were over. On the evening of the 5th of June he was thrown into the cell at the barracks of Yugoslav People's Army. There he lay unconscious for two hours. No one helped him, so he died in the presence of all prisoners in that cell. His body lay at the city mortuary until the 9th of June, when I succeeded, by the influence of my relatives from Titograd, where I came seven days before my husband was murdered, to get permission for taking over his body at Čekrčići. During the taking over of his body, Muslims attacked us from Kula with all the arms they had, so the taking over was hardly carried out. I demanded a medical checkup of the corpse because I knew that it was a crime and Muslims from Visoko would try to hide it with the story of my husband's "suicide."
- There were dreadful head injuries.
- Large swellings and bloody bruises covered the body, one ear was almost cut off, the skull was broken behind the ear.
- He was unstitched under the neck to scapula.
- The skin was dark because of contusions and bloody bruises.

It did not appear to be suicide.

Svetomir was buried on the 10th of June 1992 at the Čekrčići graveyard. I collected all the facts about his suffering and delivered them to The Commission for Investigation of War Crimes. I exposed all these facts on Radio Ilijaš, Radio Belgrade and to two British reporters.

The eyewitnesses of the capture and taking away testified about the crime. I had talked with them. Their statements can be found at The National Security Service at Ilijaš, where they were interrogated after coming out of Visoko. Other Muslim prisoners have also testified to the crime after they were exchanged. Eyewitnesses of Svetomir's death and his torture were Duško Nikolić, Jovan Bilal, Risto Cvijetić, Zoran "Čićo" Vukičević, Trifko Cvjetković, Simo from Ozrakovići and many others.

My husband was arrested and led away by Samir Halilović called Sane, Gipsy, who was employed at Vitez; Džemo Sjedić, Gipsy, who was employed at the Čatići power plant and lived at Luke; and one more who was a former policeman at police service and who activated himself at the beginning of war. He wore a helmet and was masked. I found out that he was from Seoce. He conducted the capture and ransacking of our apartment. Arms and membership card of Serbian Democratic Party were well-hidden. They didn't find that, but they found a big knife used for preparing food for winter and a cable for checking motor oil level, which they declared to be a rope for choking. On the basis of those facts they declared my husband to be a Chetnik Vojvoda. They planted a list of names in his house and blamed it on him so they could arrest him. Allegedly they were Chetniks from Visoko. At the police station my husband was beaten by Tufo Buza and investigators Asim Hamzić and Mrčo Halilović. At barracks he was beaten again by Samir Selimović and Abdula Karić. He was half-dead and thrown into the cell where he died two hours later. The next day Muslims fabricated the story of my husband's suicide to hide their crime.

They robbed our apartment and took our car away.

On Radio Visoko, Muslims answered back to an accusation that I brought against them on Radio Ilijaš. They stated that it was an inadmissible accident made by extremists that would be punished, but they were not those whose names I had quoted. That denial demonstrated their fear of testifying and their wish to hide actual criminals. Therefore everyone who knows anything should speak up and quote the names. The criminals have to know that their crimes are not unknown and that they will be responsible for them.

Tomka Vujisić

DUSKO RAKOVIĆ, son of JOVA
Born on the 22nd of May 1958, at Sarajevo
Visoko, Maurovic, 38
(Now resides in Portland, Maine)

During May and June our representatives and representatives of former Territorial Defence Forces of Visoko conducted negotiations. At that time we could make an agreement easily because they still were not well armed. As soon as they became armed, they attacked us. On the 17th of June, the representatives from Territorial Defence Forces from Visoko came to our village to negotiate. The leader of the group was Ismet Graho, a former member of Yugoslav People's Army, and later he joined Territorial Defence Forces. He was born at Doboj. He came with:

• Hasib and Hasan Mušinbegović, two brothers who were former members of Yugoslav People's Army. The Mušinbegovićs were our neighbors from the next village,

Kološići. That day Hasib Mušinbegović spent time mostly talking with local villagers. He told them that he would never be a member of an ethnic army;

• Faik Dlakić, nicknamed Keko, a teacher in our local community for twelve years, who played football for our football team. He lived in the next village, Bradve;

• Hasan Hadžiosmanović a teacher of the philosophy of Marxism, defense and protection technics. He lived in our community and also played football for our football team.

All of them and the majority of other Muslims were protesting when they heard of our intention to migrate. They asserted that it was not necessary. They persuaded us that our fear was groundless and that we ought to deliver one part of our arms only. They advised us to establish only one Serbian troop, which would be a part of Territorial Defence Forces and would act at our local community.

Hasib and Hasan Mušinbegović lived in the house next to the Vuković family, whose members were killed during arrest. Families of Damjanović and Ristić, who lived at village Hlapčevići, were also killed. Only one member of the Damjanović family survived. That was Zoran, although he suffered seven injuries.

They surrounded and attacked us about six o'clock in the morning and killed five of our men: Rajko Raković, Višnja Bajić, Dragan Cvijetić, Igor Stojčić and Vlatko Milanović. They attacked us with a few thousand soldiers and heavy artillery. We didn't have those kind of arms but only about sixty shotguns to protect the village. After we had realized that we were not able to offer resistance, we decided to negotiate with the Muslims.

Our three negotiators—Milorad Cvjetić and Milenko and Bogdan Milanović—went to their location. When they came back they told us that there would be no problems. All we had to do was to lay down our arms and to make statements at a nearby school.

We gathered shotguns at the yard of Ilija Vanovac and went to the Muslim location, where they had waited for us. There we loaded our arms onto their cars. They put us onto trucks and we left on our trip to uncertainty. During the arrest and on our way to the barracks we experienced many troubles and were beaten. They locked us into a cellar where we stayed for one hour. Then people wearing uniforms came. They sat down in front of the cellar door and began to take our biographical data. One of them was Zijad Kadrić, whom I knew personally. Later I realized that he was the administrator of the camp. When my turn came, he told me not to be afraid and that everything would be put in order. After we had given our data, we went into other room, already occupied by 160 men.

During two days we did not know if we were more thirsty or hungry, because they didn't give us anything. After two days they started to bring one meal daily. They didn't beat us at first because we had to be exchanged with inhabitants of one Muslim village from Ilijaš district. But that exchange was unsuccessful and troubles began. As a normal human being I was not able to understand such repulsive things that one man can do to another. I thought that it was possible only in well directed films.

As there were 160 men in one room, we were lying on the floor. We were not able to stretch our legs, so many of us slept twisted or sitting. There were neither carpets nor blankets. As it was summertime and the room was full of people, we kept the windows open all day long. But overnight it was cold to men who slept near windows and very hot to those on the opposite side, so they hardly breathed. There were two feces cans in the room, near the door, next to the prisoners' heads. We were not aware of air pollution and dirt because no one of us had washed face and hands, not to mention bathing and tooth washing.

They supplied us with water from a hydrant in front of the barracks. One who got water without a beating was a happy man.

There were inmates who had never left the room during their stay at the camp. One inmate had constipation for sixty days. Guards put bread and food for us onto the floor, as if we were animals. The food was in mess kits. There was one meal for five or six persons at one dish. Some of us got meals on the covers. We had no spoons. Dishes went from one mouth to another. The same dishes were used after that at three rooms more, without washing.

At camp there were prisoners aged sixteen to eighty. Ten inmates were over eighty. After forty days, the Muslims began to release those who were old and ill and who already were on their deathbed. We took our first bath after forty days.

The cell door had locks and keys, but guards strengthened it with more iron and padlocked it. We were also guarded by five or six wardens.

There were 160 men in our room, but there would be a place for 160 prisoners more when we heard the padlock strike the iron. Every time a warden came into the room, someone got a beating. It was good to be beaten in the room, because wardens were beating with sticks and fists. But there was special equipment for physical punishment in the cellar: bolts, various handles, metal pipes . . .

They began to take us to dig trenches, where we were beaten, too. They formed an alleged investigation board for diggers. They used to take one of us out of the trench. Then they started to punish us; they would beat our backs with two handles and if one fell down they went on kicking his ribs and loins with heavy soldier's boots. After that they began to investigate. They asked which kind of arms we had and who had given the arms to us. They shook our pockets and took away our watches, money, necklaces. The robbery was the real aim of their investigation. Then they would start from the beginning. Two wardens were shooting and beating the rest of us to enable us to see what "the investigators" were doing. After beatings, some of our people were not able to walk anymore, so we carried them into the room.

I took part in digging trenches several times. The last time I was there, I was injured. It was the 17th of June 1992. We were working at the entrance of Visoko, near an old gasoline pump, two hundred meters air line far from the location of Serbian troops. Those who had been working the day before told us that no one was beaten and that there was enough food. Next day when the Muslims asked who wanted to go for work, we all signed up. One of the wardens came in and chose some of us. Every time when we went to work, two or three wardens were going with us to watch over us. That morning they came unusually early, about seven o'clock.

We went out in line, with wardens in front and behind us. We were crossing the sniper field. One warden told us to bend and run for fifty to sixty meters and we would be safe again. When we had come to the location where we had to work, the wardens told us that they had to go and the policemen from a nearby location were ordered to watch over us. We started to carry out their orders. Two hours later two men in uniforms came to us. They had taken a dummy grenade launcher from a nearby magazine. They asked if we had experience with it. Some of us came forward to explain to them what to do. They put a grenade into the rifle, took aim at the barracks and fired. After that they gave us some cigarettes and went away. In the meantime both Muslims and Serbs were firing a lot. Young soldiers came again and told us to move into the trench until the firing ceased. We smoked two or three cigarettes. The same boys returned and ordered us to go on with digging. Five to ten minutes later I became conscious. I saw I was lying on the ground. I didn't know what had happened.

When I turned around I saw people lying in trenches full of blood puddles. I felt as if my shoulder was broken off. Then I saw the others. When I heard their screaming, "Dule, help me! Dule, I'm dying!" I stopped thinking about myself. Three of fifteen of us diggers were seriously injured. They were Sladjan Šljivić, Saša Milanović, and Branivoj Radulović. Minor injuries had gotten Duško Raković, Milenko Despotović, Stojko Krsmanović, Jovo Krsmanović, Željko Šljivić and Dalibor Glišić. Those who were not injured were Jovo Milanović, Boban Vojnović, Ratko Đukić, Manojilo Vanovac, Mirko Kuvač and Zoran Topalović.

All these facts—that we had no wardens as usual, the shooting of a dummy rifle grenade (probably to determinate the coordinates and distance) prove that the grenade came from the Muslim rather than from the Serbian side.

Five to six minutes after the explosion, we were driven to hospital. Three inmates with serious injuries got the first aid at Visoko and after that they were driven to Zenica. Six of us also got first aid at the hospital. Then we were driven back to the barracks dispensary.

At the hospital at Visoko, something very unpleasant happened to me. While we were waiting for first aid I saw my fellow worker, Nijaz Ćelebić, called Kize. We were good friends. Before the war, he asked me to be his godfather and vice versa. He told me, "If Chetnik come you will protect me, and if the Ustashe (Croats) come I shall protect you and your family." I was very glad when I saw him at hospital. But in the presence of all the physicians and nurses he attacked me as if I were the worst extremist.

After we were driven back to the barracks, they put us in the attic where the dispensary was located. Two days after we had arrived there, the main investigator, Asim Hamzić, and the mayor of Visoko, Kenan Jusufbašić, visited us. They told us that some TV reporters had to come so we had to be careful of what we spoke about. TV reporters came and we made statements. We stayed at this dispensary from the 17th of June to the 17th of August 1992.

After we had spent about fifty days at the concentration camp, Muslims allowed our families to visit us. Up to that time we had no any information about our children and wives who had stayed at home. We had no idea what had happened with our property. When the visitors came, we heard that our children and wives were taken to the next village. We could not take into our room anything that our visitors brought for us.

Visits occurred on fixed days. It was common that the strongest firing took place during the visit. Territorial Defense Forces had two guns near the barracks and they used to fire at Serbs who were about two hundred meters away from the barracks.

If the Serbs answered back with firing, the Muslims would say that our Chetniks were shooting at us and our visitors. A few grenades had hit the building directly and killed two inmates: Milo Krunić and Trifko Glišić. More than twenty inmates got injured.

Ten men at least died in the concentration camp, and their deaths were the consequence of beating, hunger and grenades (they, as I said, caused the death of two men), and more than thirty were wounded. Nobody knows how many inmates had been beaten up.

We were moved from dispensary to temporary custody, where we stayed for thirty days. There we couldn't go out. We could only go to the corridor where we got our meals. Two wardens always were staying with rifles aimed at the prisoners while we were eating. Smoking was permitted only after meals, so we could smoke only three or four cigarettes daily. From temporary custody we were driven into Zenica prison. Those were better living conditions; we were less beaten but often more hungry. There were two meals daily. They consisted of rice soup with two or three pieces of unpeeled potato. There were no fat or spices. Several times we spent some days without bread or without both soup and bread. The longest period without a meal and bread lasted for twelve days. If there had been no visitors or the priest who worked at Zenica, most of us would have died because of hunger or diseases.

Here are the names of those who took part in these events:

• Kenan Jusufbašić, the mayor of Visoko, who was informed about anything that had happened; he was also informed about the murdered, beaten and deceased men;

• Srečko Kitić, the president of the municipal court, who had sent us to Zenica as we were "extremists and Chetniks";

• Asim Hamzić, the main investigator, former policeman, who was the initiator of those events;

• Mrčo Halilović, Hamzić's deputy who carried out every project of Hamzić's. He hit and mistreated a lot of inmates. He had some subordinates who carried out even the most severe directives. I can remember some of them: Jasmin Pinjić, called Pinč, Fejzić, called Daidža, Miralem Čengić, Dizdar, Burko Šačir.

• The prison administrator also belonged to this quasi elite. He was informed about physical punishment and robbery. He is responsible for all those who were murdered and deceased at the camp.

• Nisat Ramić and his men had executed members of the Vuković, Ristić and Damjanović families. They also robbed many houses.

We were expelled and robbed only because we were

Serbs. I have lost a house, business office, a Golf diesel car and fifteen dulums plot (four acres of land).

Duško Raković

ILIJA VANOVAC, son of NEDO
Born on the 20th of October 1949 at Đindići
Lived at village Maurovići, Visoko
Died several years ago in Brčko, Bosnia

On the 20th of June 1992 at 6:30 a.m. our village was attacked from all sides. The enemy used infantry arms and later mortar shells and guns. The first victims had fallen. They were Vlatko Milanović, Igor Stojčić, Dragan Cvijetić (Branko) and Višnja Bajić. Everything was over by 10:30 a.m. The calm was broken off at 11 a.m. They used a megaphone to ask us to surrender at once and to make our statements at the school at Donje Moštre. That place was about two kilometers from our village. If we didn't, they would destroy and burn everything and everyone.

Our staff for critical situations negotiated and agreed with the other side to stop hostility. We believed in it. But things took an unexpected turn. We found ourselves in an unenviable situation. They sent a message to us that they would murder, burn and destroy everything if we rejected capitulation. I believed they would carry out their threat. So we surrendered to the Muslims. We believed that we only had to make statements at the school. Some of us thought and spoke in a different way. We decided to surrender and save our families.

Delivery took place about 1 p.m. They led us to the next Muslim village, Bradve. They lined us up on the road. We stayed there for two hours. They searched us and took away things that they were interested in. They started to provoke us, as we were Chetniks, etc. Some rabbles with wrapped heads aimed their rifles at us. They told us that they came from Vukovar and other Croatian places. I saw Branko Janjušić. His head was bleeding. One soldier broke it with a rifle butt. We were wondering what had happened to us. We realized that we were wrong. Everything was over. They put seventy of us onto an FAP truck, which was stolen from Vukan Kuprešak, and drove us to Ahmed Fetahagić barracks at Visoko, seven kilometers from my village.

We were thrown into the barracks cellar, where they took our data. After that, somebody issued the command and we moved to the second floor, into room No. 3. Soldiers who were staying outside on the stairway struck some of us. At room No. 3 we found people from Kalotići and other villages.

I saw Dejan Mičanović. His head was wrapped and bloody. Gojko Duvnjak's hand was broken while being taken to prison. We sat down on the floor. The room was as full as a box of matches. Somebody counted men in the rooms. There were about 140, and after two days 154 inmates in a space of forty square meters. One could sit in some way, but there was no way to lie down. I thought about the good luck of those who got placed along the wall. They could lean against it. My place was in the middle of the crowd. We were silent, sitting down, looking around, greeting one another with glances and gentle smiles.

Night fell. Somebody was interested in dinner, the others asked for water. There was neither dinner nor water. A warden brought two feces cans. Nothing happened. Some inmates were whispering, another stared at one point, some of us fell asleep, while the others lay down on the floor. Everything seemed to be all right and calm, up to the moment when the lights were turned off. People stirred, everybody wanted to lay down, but that was impossible. Some of us had not enough space; one could hear advice: "Do not lay on your back but on your side, you need less space." Lots of inmates were sitting all night long—some of them because of pride, the others just couldn't sleep. Night passed calmly.

The next day began without breakfast. The Muslims called for Nenad Vanovac and Miloš Milanović, a teacher. Nenad was charged for possessing arms and Miloš was accused of being a sniper. This man was intereseted in books; he had never taken a rifle in his hands. Miloš returned two hours later. He could hardly stand on his feet. He was severely beaten. Nenad was beaten up in the evening. They wanted him to say where the guns, mortars and other kinds of arms were. He confessed nothing, because we had no arms of that kind.

I mention here that the investigative room was below our room so we could hear every scream and every blow. It was sad that healthy and innocent people were beaten. More depressing was the fact that we all belonged to the same family and we were from the same village. We were all brothers, cousins, godfathers, friends, so our hearts were broken when one of us was mistreated. Miloš' brothers and relatives and Nenad's three brothers, brother-in-law, uncles, father-in-law and other relatives could hear their screaming and sufferings. That day passed and we were overwhelmed by grief and pain. The whole night long we were putting cold wet compresses on their bodies. We were unable to see their injuries until the morning. Their backs were dark as a coal; their bodies were covered by bruises up to the hands. Both Miloš and Nenad were immobile.

The next day wardens took away Nenad again. He couldn't walk, so two of them carried him up. He was beaten again and lost consciousness. A few hours later they returned him to the room. He was half-dead. He spent fifteen days lying on the bare floor. Some of his ribs were broken.

The next day Saša Krsmanović was called. New screams and sufferings came after. They led him away and beat him seven times. His father was weeping in our room and pulled his hair out. Nenad's grandfather, uncle and other inmates became speechless from horror. The same thing repeated the next days.

This was happening in all rooms. Investigation lasted for twenty days. Many of our people had broken arms and legs.

After twenty days the Muslims gave to us one meal daily. One dish contained food for five men and on its cover there was a meal for two prisoners. Hunger and fights broke out. Anyone who came to the barracks could enter our room. There were soldiers, casualties, soldiers form Croatian troops—all of them were venting their fury on us. Every evening wardens were taking people away and beating them in corridors. They were free to do anything they wanted. The situation was horrible. There was hell in the camp. Chaos began, people were talking about events. Optimists turned into pessimists. Nobody was sure if he would stay alive.

The barracks lay on the target of both Serbian and Muslim troops. Muslims had put their two guns behind the barracks and from there they shot Serbs. Serbs were looking for the Muslim guns, so their grenades were falling around the barracks. Shell fragments were crashing into rooms through windows. We were helpless, waiting for a grenade to crash into our room. This continued through three and a half months while I was at Visoko. During calm periods the Muslims were beating us, just to vent their fury. We were beaten days and nights, up to midnight. Wardens were riding inmates and crying: "Giddyup, Chetnik!" We were together with our fathers, old men of eighty-six. Muslims captured everyone. Not one Serb stayed at the village. Women and children were led into the next village, Hlapčevići. They stayed there for eight days. We were talking with old men who had survived the First and Second World War. Some of them were prisoners under the Germans (my father for two years). This situation was worse. Germans were cultured. They did not torture their prisoners.

One day we started to dig trenches. Someone said, "It's lunch at two!" That was the only meal for twenty-four hours. About ten wardens and soldiers took pickax handles and started to beat all of us on our backs and shoulders. They were crying, "Hurry up!" and scolding us. Beside the trench, beneath the tree there were three men who investigated us one by one. They asked what kind of arms we had, what we had in our pockets, on our wrists. We had to take out anything they wanted. Total robbery and beating began. Men were losing consciousness. That evening we were not able to move. Boro Raković could not stand on his feet for twenty-five days. We were carrying him in a blanket.

The next day a new group of inmates was taken out. They had the same experience. The situation was getting worse and worse every day. I had various thoughts in my mind. I was thinking about suicide. The situation seemed to be unbearable. I had thought that physical punishment was a matter of investigation and each warden's self-will. But I saw that the main people of the camp warden Zijo Kadrić and main investigator Asim Hamzić were watching our sufferings from the windows. My mind was full and I asked myself what had they intended, if they wanted to exhaust us, to kill us or wash our brains to manipulate us easier?

Forty days later the Muslims released old men. My father, who was seventy, was free. I felt relief. That meant one trouble less. Two brothers of mine and I stayed at the camp. My younger brother Mane was in the same room with me, while Ratko was in the next room. I heard that he was beaten, too, and I was more upset by that than by my own suffering. We became accustomed to grenades and guns. The firing was quite normal for us. I convinced myself by saying, "He sleeps so deeply that gunfire could not awaken him." Some people were able to sleep and snore during furious shooting. They were, for example, Novica Milanović and Rajko Topalović. They were sleeping near me, so I remembered them.

After fifty days of my imprisonment my wife visited me. I could never forget that day. It was like a dream, as if we had not seen each other for fifty years. I was confused. I tried to concentrate. At the visiting room one could only hear weeping. I also felt the need to weep, but when I saw tears all around me, I restrained myself. I came calmly to my wife to show her that everything was all right and that she had no reason to cry. I asked her about the children, parents, of events at the village. She told me that all of them felt well. According to her answer I could see how well they were. She was pale and her chin was shivering. I knew that I had nothing to ask and must not ask her anything. It was important to me that we all were healthy. I only advised them to go to Serb territory if it would be possible. Not one of our Muslim friends had tried to help her. I asked myself why. *Where did I make a mistake? Maybe I did not know to demonstrate my favor?* I asked myself. I could not believe that none of the Osmanović, Halač, Vrače or Valjevac families had responded.

We had always been together, truly friends, we had visited one another. Now it was over. How? Why? Still I think that we were the victims of politics that we met with. Maybe they must not turn to my family to ask them anything, to instill in them faith and certainty. That was very painful for me.

But when I saw that the same thing had happened to all neighbours, I understood that something more important had occurred. Actual authorities at Visoko had proclaimed us the worst criminals.

Someone believed them; the others respected executive command. That was the reason for the heartlessness of my neighbours and Muslim friends. Let it be the matter of their honesty and humanity. Nevertheless, I hope God will save them. Let them live in their own peace if they could find it or get it from God.

I said goodbye to my wife. She wept. The commander of the shift, Šačir, was scolding her because she was crying. There was allegedly no reason for tears. He almost hit her. He could not understand why we were weeping. He would, if this had happened to him. If he were a human being he would never stop weeping because he had feigned to be a hero over helpless Serb citizens of Visoko.

The visit was over. My wife brought everything: bread, meat, pie. I had only one wish—to eat and then I could die. It would be a pity to die hungry. But after I was fed, I did not want to die, although death was always in my mind. We heard that nine men died after they were beaten in the cellar. One thought that the same thing would happen to him, because Muslims continued to terrorize, to take people away, beat and investigate them. Then my turn came again. After inspection, that is after we were re-sorted to rooms, I was ordered to go to room No. 4. It was an infamous room. They put alleged extremists there. All the camp's personnel were looking at room No. 4.

Guard Eso Genjac called me. I had to scrub three floors. When I finished he told me that we just had met. The same evening I was called to go to the closet. Four guards started to beat me with hands and feet. After they harmed me, they asked for money. I said I had no money, but they called me a liar, because I had a private practice before the war. They threatened to kill me and told me to think about money. One of them was "Pinć" Genjac. The rest of them were unknown to me. The same thing repeated three times more. Beating, asking for money . . . I thought my life was over. I was mad. Whenever it was their shift I knew what would happen to me.

But in spite of all those troubles something good happened to me. I was called to trial. It lasted for three months at Visoko and we were moved into the cellar. I was very glad to go down and to get out of hell.

It was much better in the cellar. We had three small meals daily. There was neither beating nor torture. There was still hell in the upper rooms. Three days after my coming to the cellar, on the 5th of September 1992 some grenades hit the barracks. One of them hit room No. 4 where I had been earlier. It was horrible. There were fifteen inmates with serious or minor injuries. Trifko Glišić and Milo Krunić were killed. Vojno Raković died—because the warden Muste Dedić struck him while he was heading with him to the ambulance to get medical aid. Milivoj Bajić also was murdered when a stray bullet came through the window. One man from Goruša village also died. He had just arrived and was beaten, and he succumbed to his wounds.

In the cellar cells there were about forty prisoners. We spent about one month there. The cellar was moist, there was no sunlight, but I was happy to be there. I repeated thanks to God. Slowly I relaxed and all the events from the upper floor streamed through my mind. I saw pictures of events: how Muslims beat Jovo Ljepić and rode him, shouting, "Giddyup, Chetnik"; there were Vukan Kuprešak, Trifko Glišić and Skopljak Živko and many others. Every week new prisoners came into the cellar.

People from International Red Cross came here. They registered all of us. They instilled in us some hope to survive. One month later my wife and my mother visited me. Mother hardly was able to come. Her gallbladder was bad, but she wanted to see me. While they were coming here, two women (Nevenka Raković and Mladen's Mediha) were injured. Their situation was worse than ours. They were the heroes; they were passing under rain of fire to bring something for us not to die of hunger. On the 1st of October 1992, I was sent to Zenica, where I stayed up to April 1994, when I was exchanged.

Ilija Vanovac

Transcript of a letter by Velimir Mirković
Received from Germany in August 1999

VELIMIR MIRKOVIĆ
Westfalen Str.55
37671 Luchtringen
GERMANY

Dear Mr. Milanović,

After a rather long period I found some free time to write these few words to you. My best regards to all of you, I wish you all the best. I also wish to thank you for everything you have done for me. The book was crown evidence at the court, so the judges brought positive decision in regard to my further stay here in Germany. Will that be the final solution, nobody knows, but it is anticipated that about 20,000 people from Bosnia will get the right to stay in Germany. There is nothing new here, except that I have learned where Mrčo has been hiding, so I called him and said that he would have "to pay the bill" for everything he had done at the camp of Visoko. After that he changed his address and phone number, but other men are on his trail. I looked for all of them through the computer and there is no problem to find where they are. But the problem is that those from the Hague are not interested in catching up with them and condemning them for their crimes.

I revert now to what I promised to write to you about. Many

are those who think that everything is forgotten, but when one starts speaking about it, the images arise by themselves.

I was arrested by Muslim's Territorial Defense on June 9, 1992, at around 3 or 4 p.m. I was taken to the school where they had their headquarters and where I found the men with whom I have lived all through my childhood, went to school, worked. There were about forty of them and I heard the question, "Where did you find that *Chetnik*? Take him away, and show him what he will get!" From Podvinci I was transferred for examination to Grančanica by the car of Mirče Radosavljević, which was confiscated, and all the time they were driving it in the first gear with hand brakes on. Then the beating started. The welcome at Grančanica was the same as at Podvinci, plus the beating. I was interrogated by Suljo Husić, the teacher, Hamdo Halilović, the driver, (commanding officer of the Terr. Defense of Grančanica), as well as by four employees of the local police of Visoko. I was beaten by Halilović and Hasic, the cook at the school of Grančanica, whose first names I don't remember but whose faces I will never forget, by Hajlovac, the hunter, and by others. Later, they threw water over me to get me out of the coma and when I came to my senses I saw the blood on the floor and on the walls. Then Mrčo gave me a hard blow on my head with his automatic rifle. He was aiming with his rifle butt at my forehead, but I evaded the blow. On that occasion the rifle frame caught my face and I started bleeding. The other two men standing at the sides continued beating me all the time until Halilović got up and signaled them to stop. Then they dragged me away to the movie theater hall where other men from Goruša, Podvinci and other Serbian villages were already brought in, in total about sixty-five men. All those who were not taken for the examination immediately were taken there later on and during the night. All lights down, you don't know who know is who, and you are not allowed to say anything. Around two hours past midnight we moved to the barracks of Visoko where a "welcome" was organized for us by Green Berets (green berets have been worn by Muslim soldiers) and they were in undershirts already splashed with blood. We all had to pass through a double row of men who kept mistreating us. They threw us first in the basement and from there we were sent to separate rooms. Mine was the room No. 1 with the first prisoners already there: Živko Skopljak, Slobodan Gogić, Samardžić and others. About ten to fifteen people were set apart and piled together in room No. 1, while our torturers were preparing instruments for beating: sticks, wooden handles, hammers (of two kilograms) and various other devices. In that room there were from Grančanica: Risto Kokoruš, Ranko Kokoruš, Vera Dundić, Milo Kokoruš, myself and some others, too. They kept beating us day and night without stopping. Asim Hamzić used to come to the room trying to persuade men that nothing would happen to them, that they should only hand over their arms and tell where the radio stations were located (we didn't have them at all). Men from Kralup, Buci, Banjer were brought in and later on, around June 15, 1992, also the inhabitants of Podvisoko. At one moment the policemen in blue uniforms were charged to look after us so the army members were not allowed to enter the room and beat us. That happened after an intervention of Mulo Hodžić, director of KTK Visoko, who was an influential person at Visoko. But Hamzić and Halilović grabbed every opportunity to take out prisoners past midnight and beat them. So on June 15, 1992, they took out Jovo Marić at about half past midnight for the "examination" and brought him back at 5:30 a.m. They had asked him to calculate the coordinates of certain peak elevations in the territory of Ilijaš, because they had nobody trained to do that, and they needed coordinates for bombing Serbian positions. I was already acquainted with Jovo and his brother, as we used to work in the same company. We had to tear up our shirts in order to put wet compresses on his body. We thought he couldn't survive, but somehow we managed to save him from death. After three to four days he took his first piece of bread, because until then he was unable to swallow and he had a high fever, but wet compresses helped him to stay alive.

On one occasion I was ordered to empty the garbage can from the room No. 1: "Head down, don't look aside! If you give a glance you will get beaten!" By chance there happened to be a road carrier, a good man, and he asked me whether I needed something. I asked for his permission to look for some bottles in order to bring water to the prisoners. He gave me his permission but asked me to bring the water first to the people kept in the basement about whom we didn't know anything. I saw then what was awaiting us. I saw in one corner Živko Skopljak, who was hardly recognizable, and on the other side, tied up to the radiator, Risto Kokoruš, his face misshapen, Jovo Ljepić, and Zoran Vukićević and some other men, tortured beyond recognition. The room was covered with blood. The cans that I was taking out were filled with blood drying already on the top. Zoran Vukićević told me then that he had to eat one lock of his own hair that they had pulled out. In the basement we were 145 and later on, without women and children, 410 in total. Before I was released I knew all the men from the basement so when we were making lists, Jovica Đukić said that I knew all those who were there from the first day.

With bringing people from Radovlje, Poriječani, Mulići, Kalotići and Liješeva, the same treatment continued on and on. We dug trenches for the needs of Balyas (Muslim trash) on the barracks ground, where Mrčo with his acolytes would take us. We were beaten as the dogs and few are those who could say that they haven't been beaten at all. I remember that Jovica Đukić said that he was stabbed with a knife in his stomach and legs, and his shoes were filled with blood and the clothes all soaked through.

Every piece of money, gold, watches and everything that had some value was taken from us. After thirty-seven days, we were allowed to take our first bath. Five minutes in all, and see what you can wash! We dug twenty trenches on barracks ground, and later we had to pick up wood for them, to repair roads at Visočica, to dig trenches and do some other things too, while, at the same time, beating and interrogations continued.

Once I had to distribute food to people, and I did it only once and never again. Hungry men fought for a piece of bread or a sip of water. There were people who never went to the toilets, up to fifty-two days in the case of Janko Todorović. Every time they had a failure at the front, and there were many, we had to pay at a "high price." Once, while digging trenches, Srpko Dundić was beaten up so that he lost his sight. We needed to consult with a doctor but the mere idea had frightened us. Then the manager Zijad Kadrić gave us a few tablets, and we had to carry Boro Toljević to the ambulance. I saw then that there wasn't a spot on his body which didn't bear the blues.

But men had to endure.

In August we had the visit of people from the International Red Cross who, seeing where we had been sleeping, made some remarks to the warden of the camp, which the guards used as a pretext to beat us, as supposedly we had been complaining. By the end of August, Milorad Jovičić came to the camp; shortly afterwards Mrdići, as well as Samojko Bosiljčić, my neighbour, and Božo Stojanović, who was once taken prisoner and released, but brought in again because he tried to transfer his property, sheep and cattle with the aid of the Croats to Kiseljak. He succeeded in it, but when he came back to pick up his wife he was arrested for the second time.

In September 1992, around September 11, the room in which I was kept with some other forty-five men was struck with two shells. The first shell fell under the window so that the dust rose and somebody cried not to stand up as a second shell was coming. An explosion followed and we couldn't see anything.

Somebody in the panic managed to break down the door and we came running into the anteroom. From the room came out the first wounded people, their blood running down. Wounded were Ljepić Vojislav, Đukić Jovica, Milorad Jovičić, Dabić Rajko, Jovo Milanović . . . I came back to the room to see what happened to the others. In the anteroom there were lying down Trifko Glišić—dead, Samojko Bosiljčić—heavily wounded; Nikola Šarenac was taken out by Rade Šarenac and Nikica Todorović. In the room we found Milija Krunić, but every assistance was too late for him as he had a lethal wound on the head, smashed with shell fragments.

At the return from the hospital of Nikola Šarenac and of the other heavily wounded men, we were transferred to the first floor where we had a lot to do, cleaning wounds, washing clothes and bandaging the wounded. The most risky matter for us was to accompany wounded prisoners to the health center, because at the same time they had been bringing their wounded soldiers from the war fields, they vented their rage at us. I remember clearly all those people, but by helping the wounded men I escaped the visits of Mrčo and of his acolytes.

But what had to happen, had to happen. After some time we were sent to separate rooms. I was with Jovo Milanović again and I continued bandaging his hand. Winter was approaching and there was no news about our release. Out of the blue came the visit of the Red Cross, asking us whether we were interested in going to Montenegro. Of course we responded all favourably to this invitation, but we had to wait long so we started losing hope that we would be liberated at all. We continued on chopping wood at Kondžilo for the needs of the Muslim army, hoping, however, that we would somehow be released. When on December 23, 1992, we saw on barracks ground the blue helmets and the delegation of the Red Cross from Geneva, we knew that our pains would end. When leaving the camp I managed to take out the complete list of camp inmates that I drew at the camp of Visoko. I was the last to leave the room with my luggage, hiding between my shirts the booklet with the inventory and the list. Behind me there were two soldiers with blue helmets, so the fear left me. The fear I felt was because we knew that what was written would be "paid back double." But in all that chaos I had the chance that allowed me to be free after not sleeping the last two nights, thinking about whether I should bring that list with me or destroy it.

Via Zenica-Mostar-Ploče, we were transferred to Herceg Novi. It was unthinkable, but well, it happened! What happened once, should it never happen again! By the end of January I left Montenegro with a passport provided by the Red Cross. From that day on to the present day I live and work in Germany with my family.

I think that we all had about the same difficulties and problems after leaving the camp. Imsomnia, bad dreams, the images from the camp coming back to me during three years after my release from the camp. Even presently I see these images in my dreams, because it cannot ever be forgotten nor could it be pardoned to our oppressors for all that is so deeply registered in our memory.

With this letter I am sending you a copy of the list of the camp inmates that I have saved so you could compare it with the list published in the book and make some corrections.

My regards to the camp inmates that you meet and who are living in the United States. If you need anything else please contact me.

Best regards to all from Velo
Signed, Velimir Mirković

DORDJO "DORDO" MILANOVIĆ, son of OSTOJA
Kalotići No.3, Visoko
Bosnia and Herzegovina
(Now resides at Saint Petersburg, Florida)

On June 20, 1992, at 6 a.m. an attack of Muslim's Territorial Defense was performed against Serbian settlements in the community of Visoko. On that occasion all men, whether capable for the army or not, from the age of fifteen up, women, children, even old women, were taken to the local centres to be released after seven to ten days. When women with children came home they were stunned with the view. Houses were completely destroyed, robbed. Everything that had some value was taken out, so women and children were compelled to leave their homes. Women and children were leaving in tears, not knowing where to go, in what direction to go.

On that dark day of the 20th of June, my son Siniša and myself were sleeping at home when we heard shooting around the place. We got up quickly and climbed upstairs to the attic. I had with me a 7.62 mm pistol and two bombs. I said to my son not to worry as I was pretty sure that at the moment nobody would climb up to the attic and search there. We heard loud noise around the house, shouting to us to come out or otherwise they would launch a Wasp (a sort of weapon). As I was watching them through a small opening in the attic, I saw that they hadn't any Wasp but a burst was fired on the roof and on the windows of the attic. My son and I remained silent when windows and doors burst open, being broken down. Noise and screams were heard. They were yelling, asking whether there was anybody at home. We kept silent while they were knocking over everything in the house. I saw them leaving the house carrying the video cassette recorder, TV set and other things they liked. All the men (Serbs) were lined up and they were pushing them, striking them with feet, hands and gun butts. Some of the men I saw were tied with wire. They were beating them. Children and women followed. Tears, shrieks, children screaming. In twenty minutes the life left the village of Kalotići. My son and I were watching silently the row of women and children slowly moving. A tomblike silence fell on the village. After some thirty minutes we heard the roaring of cows and loud barking of tied dogs as if they knew that they would not get any food or water that day. A few fired shells silenced the dogs for a while. I was thinking what to do, because I was sure that we shouldn't leave the house that same day, as too many soldiers were around our village. I said to my son that we should stay in the attic until dark or until the morning the next day. The time was passing, eleven o'clock already, and it was becoming too hot in the attic. I told my son to slip noiselessly to the kitchen in order to bring us water. He brought two litres of water and so we remained there. At 11:30 we heard the noise of a car. It was a Zastava 101 passing through the whole length of the street moving to the other end of the village. As from the attic I was capable of seeing everything, I saw the car stopping in front of the house of

Vaso Mičanović. Two men from the car entered the house, then came out carrying various things. Then they entered the next house and so from one house to the other they were taking out everything that was interesting to them. When they approached my house I recognized Meho Omanović, nicknamed Krbulja (our neighbour from the settlement of Bradve with an automatic rifle over his chest. He was accompanied by two young men and while he was standing guard the other two were taking from the houses whatever they liked. They broke down the garage door and took out my car, a Jugo 55, one and a half years old. They loaded robbed goods in the car and while shouting gaily, they left the settlement of Kalotići. They went to the other settlement, Kamenica, to continue robbing Serbian houses. In one hour they came back to take other cars from the village, which they found in garages. They finally left and silence fell on the village as in a far west movie, when all men have been killed after shooting, and only from time to time the barking of a dog would be heard. The cattle in their stables were quiet, too, as if all living creatures in the settlement felt sorrow for what had happened that gloomy day, that Saturday June 20, in the beautiful landscape of the communities of Visoko, Kalotići, Maurovići, Radovlje, Vilenjak and other settlements with Serbian populations, situated alongside the beautiful river Radovaljka, formed by about a hundred sources of drinking water, rich in fish, especially trout. Hilly country and fertile soil stretched along both sides of the river. It was our "little paradise."

It was getting dark. How to endure and how to pass the night knowing that it would be the longest one in my life? Thoughts kept running in my head. Luckily, my wife, daughter, daughter-in-law and my grandchildren were secure in Belgrade, where they went not long before the attack on Kalotići. One half of the night passed. We fell asleep, but I awoke at 3 a.m. with dark dreams. I thought about what to do. I was speaking soundlessly to myself while my son was sleeping, and I came to a decision. At 4 a.m. I woke him up, telling him that we should go from the house into grandfather's stable, as I presumed that some of our Muslim neighbours would come in the morning to give food and water to the cattle in stables.

We came down from the attic to the ground floor quietly, noiselessly. I opened the freezer, took out a large piece of meat and gave it to our dog, Lord, who was standing by, hungry. It was the last food I gave him. I left him free to go and we went to the stable. I brought with me the pistol and two bombs. We were lying down in the straw until nine o'clock in the morning. Then we heard the murmur of voices. When I looked through wooden boards I saw four Muslim men and three Muslim women, our neighbours from the nearby village of Hlapčevići. They came into the stable, gave food and water to cattle and chickens. They were carrying cans for milking cows, and as I understood from hearing their conversation, they intended to take milk to the home where Serbian children and women were kept prisoners. In our stable there was our neighbour Midhat Ajdinović, nicknamed Mide. From the stable I whispered his name and when he saw me he was so startled that he was unable to utter a word. He kept silent for a couple of minutes. He only stared at me, wondering how it was possible that I was there.

I told him to say to his father Asim that my son and I were there, and I asked him to try to transfer us to the Serbian territory. But nothing came out of it, although we used to be good neighbours once. Instead of the transfer to the Serbian territory we were transferred to the camp of Visoko. The collection point for Serbs was at the local office—Donje Moštre. When we started from Hlapčevići toward Moštre, we were told that Vladimir Milanović, son of Radovan, was killed and left lying in the wheat field near the house of Gojko Duvnjak. From Moštre we were transported to that infamous camp into which many came but never left, as criminals killed them in the most monstrous way. We were kept in room No. 4 with eighty-four camp inmates already there. We entered the room, my son Siniša, myself and Ratko Mičanović, who was fired at during the attack and who by pure chance remained alive. Silence fell. The room was overcrowded and there was no place to sit, let alone lie down. Inside the room it was hot as hell—so hot and there was no water and nobody could even think of asking for it, because if you asked you would be beaten. In one corner of the room was a can intended for keeping urine. In the room there were young boys aged fifteen and old men of eighty-eight. Five days passed so, and then came the days of horror and dread—prison inmates were digging trenches and ditches and getting beaten. We were beaten with pickax handles, with feet, with rifle butts—and the worst of all was to see two criminals beating one man with their hands, competing for who would knock him down first. Those were Hajrudin Halilović, nicknamed Mrčo, and Amir Murtić. They had separate premises where they were taking men from the room for examination (beating). Everything lasted from June 21 till September 24, when I received the sentence of the Municipal Court of Visoko condemning me to prison because of my participation in the "enemy army"!? At Zenica I was condemned to two and a half years of prison. The most painful thing for me was that the indictment was written by the public prosecutor, Mirko Lečić, a Serb, if there was anything Serbian left in him. This "convert to Islam," together with the Ustasha (Croat) Srečko Kitić, who was the president of the court chamber at Visoko, served as a cover, enabling the Muslims to present their state and government as democratic; after a "summary trial" they were sending Serbs to the prison of Zenica. We spent there difficult and painful days without food. One day the priest Miroslav Drinčić came bringing food to us Serbs, thus saving our lives, as during a period of time we were kept up to twelve days without food. Thank you, Father Miroslav, for saving people at Zenica.

As for the Red Cross Organisation, we all were disappointed because in fact it didn't do anything to help us at Zenica. In twelve months they brought us each two packs of cigarettes Vek, one toothbrush and one soap. Very sad, indeed.

So the time was passing and the 9th of October 1993 was the day when I could expect to regain my freedom. It was the happiest day for every prisoner who was allowed to leave. That was the end of my seventeen months of imprisonment in the camps of Visoko and Zenica.

Dordo Milanović, camp inmate

ŽELJKO ŠLJIVIĆ, son of SIME
Maurovići II/20 Visoko
Bosnia and Herzegovina
(Now resides in Saint Petersburg, Florida)

My name is Željko Šljivić. I was born on April 1, 1966. I was living with my parents in the settlement of Maurovići in a family house till June 20, 1992, when we were attacked by our neighbours, the Muslims, helped by other Muslims from Zenica, Kakanj, and other surrounding settlements. My settlement was namely situated in an area with Muslim villages, and we counted in all around eighty to a hundred homes. I was working at the mint factory of Visoko till about March 1992 when this factory started dismissing Serbs, pretending that there was not enough work. Only later on did we learn that weapons and other military equipment were made in this factory. But I still believed that nothing dangerous would come out of it, as I had trusted my Muslim neighbours, with whom I had been sitting at the same desk in school, dated the girls, worked . . .

At Visoko the weapons were distributed upon the presentation of the identification card (to check whether you were Muslim or not) and our neighbours made barricades at the entry and at the exit of our settlement, pretending that it was for the sake of our security only. And so on, day by day, until negotiations started between them, Muslims, and us, Serbs.

Among the Muslims that came for negotiations was my teacher, Faik Dlakić, who, the day when we were taken prisoners, stood in front of his house watching us going in a row and telling us, "You deserve it." There was also a certain Mušimbegović, an officer in the ex-Yugoslav Army, who was assuring us that nobody would ever touch us. As an example he was citing the Vuković family, who, as he said, brought him up, as well as his brothers and sisters. But the proof that you should never trust a Muslim is that the same family, Vuković, all six of them, were shot in front of their house, as a token of gratitude for their having once helped Muslim children.

So the tension was growing from day to day until the 20th of June, 1992, when we were attacked, then taken prisoner, as we didn't have any other alternative—it was either surrender or get killed. We surrendered on the condition that they would not harm old men, women and children, but they didn't observe their promise, and when they took us—men fit for military service—they also arrested all other living Serbs. They brought old men with us to the camp, and women and children to the local centres at Hlapčevići, Buzić Mahala. They released them after about ten days when they finished robbing our homes and other properties.

So we came to the camp. Few were those believing it would ever happen. I will describe the situation at the camp by telling the sufferings of my friend Saša Krsmanović. Saša was born in 1969, and he was the one who suffered more than anybody else among us. Saša was a stout fellow about 190 centimeters tall, weighing about ninety kilograms. He was taken prisoner with his grandfather (aged about seventy-five), his father and uncle. He was the only male child in their whole family. When Mrčo—the butcher of Serbs at Visoko, brother of Sefer Halilović, at that time chief commanding officer in the Muslim army—had learned all about him, he started taking Saša out of the room and torturing him in different ways. When they were taking him from the room we would all stop talking. Somebody would make the sign of the cross, somebody would murmur to himself, "They will kill him, Turkish mother fuckers," and his grandfather, who couldn't see or hear well would ask, "Is the child back?" And nobody would answer his question; we only heard coming from the room downstairs the dull blows and screaming of my friend. My eyes would fill with tears; I was crushing my fingers, speaking to myself that if I ever came out alive I would pay them back. The father of Saša, Boško, was seated, pale as a dead man; his uncle kept sighing, sweating copiously. Sometimes between his sighs he would utter, "They are not normal, they will kill our child."

After thirty to forty minutes Saša would come back to the room—in fact he would be thrown into the room by the torturers of Mrčo's, who were cursing his Serbian mother, saying that he was a Serbian bastard, and so on. All eyes were directed at Saša while he would sit next to his father, asking for a cigarette, and his poor father Boško would put wet compresses on him, crying bitterly while looking at his son's back. I would approach Saša, asking him, "Are you OK, boy?" while he would only nod his head saying, "They will come again to pick me up." I didn't believe him, but Mrčo gave him reason. He entered the room with a smile on his face, asking Saša to come for "a little talk." He was taken again. Again we heard screams, blows, moans.

They would bring him back after the beating. Night was coming and we felt a little more at ease because they used to beat rarely during the nights. I was crawling toward Saša. We smoked half of a cigarette together, because it was the last one. I didn't speak; what could I say? Saša spoke: "Željo, they have brought Ljubinka (Saša's girlfriend, whom he married after he was released from the camp). She was mistreated, too." He stopped. After a short pause he continued speaking: "They beat me because I don't fall on the floor, and when I cannot stand anymore and when I finally fall down, they continue on, beating me with their boots." I was quiet. What could I tell him? Whatever I thought to say would be in vain. I couldn't help him. Then I "turned the record" and started talking about other things, about past times, girls, soccer . . . about things that happened in another world. Later on I retired to my place and tried to get some sleep, but in vain, as I couldn't stop thinking about Saša and how he was feeling when he knew that the following day they would come and beat him again, and if not that day then the next one for sure. As for the rest of us, we all had been beaten, but nobody like Saša Krsmanović.

I was in that room until July 17, 1992, when I was wounded by a shell together with thirteen other friends of mine, among whom there was also my brother-in-law Milenko Despotović and my cousin Sladjan Šljivić, who was a teenager, and now he is an invalid as he was heavily wounded, his lungs having received fragments of the shell. After we were wounded, we were taken to the Health Centre, improvised in the attic of the camp building. I should mention that we were wounded while digging trenches in the first line of the front, where we were taken by the Muslims.

They used to give us food one time a day in the cover of a mess kit with one slice of bread for two men. And so my father and I would look at each other, he telling me that I need more food, being younger, and if he succumbed, it wouldn't matter so much, the important thing was that I should survive. I was telling him that as I am younger, I can endure more, that he needed to eat more, and so we kept trying to persuade each other as if there was extra food and not only a handful, which was hardly enough for a newborn child, not to speak about for grown-up men. When I was wounded and transferred to the Health Centre I didn't stay anymore with my father, so I didn't have to share our pains with him. When I was feeling better, I was transferred to the basement premises, which was the prison for those expecting trial for having participated in the "enemy army" (what was that army, I wondered?) and in August 1992 I was transported to Zenica and condemned to three and a half years of prison. "Qadi (Muslim judge) is accusing you, Qadi is condemning you," because I was condemned as a Serbian soldier by a court where only Muslims were present except me, so I didn't have any defence or witnesses.

In December 1992 the six of us were transferred to stay with Muslim prisoners—deserters—and it was far easier to stay in prison with them as we had enough food and nobody was beating us. At Zenica I was in the "working unit," comprised of twelve people, Serbs from Visoko taken prisoners and condemned. We had two meals daily and two walks of half an hour each, and the rest of the time we spent in prison cells. So when I lost all hope to leave the prison alive, the happiest day in my life came—the day of the exchange of prisoners, the day of freedom that I will always celebrate as a second birthday, because it was indeed in a way a new birthday.

With me, my father, Simo Šljivić, was exchanged, too. After I left there remained in the prison of Zenica three of my neighbours, who stayed there for an extra forty days. They were the last camp inmates from my settlement. Their names are Boban Vojnović, Milorad Stojančević and Radenko Vanovac.

Željko Šljivić
Smederevska Palanka
February 19, 1995

APPENDIX

A. Biographies of Prisoners Killed in Visoko Camp

1. Milija Krunić (born: 1936) He lived in Donje Moštre—settlement Ciglana near Visoko. Pensioned forest ranger, previously employed at the company Šumarstvo, Vareš. He was living in the area populated by Muslims (90%), where he was a respected neighbour. Father of two sons: Goran and Zoran, who are employed at The Ministry of Serbian Republic. He was killed by shell explosion in room No. 4 of the prisoner camp Visoko, on September 25, 1992.

2. Milivoj "Mike" Bajić (son of Lazar) (born: September 7, 1951)   Employed at the company TE Kakanj in Čatići. Father of two sons: Ninoslav and Siniša. Lived in settlement Maurovići II. He was a football player at FC Napredak and an exemplary friend and neighbour. He lived in a village where the majority of the population were Muslim, who respected him. Killed by a sniper bullet in room No. 3, on September 24, 1992, at 7:20 p.m. He was shot in the neck and the bullet damaged the artery.

3. Vojno Raković (son of Božo) (born: 1934) Employed at the

factory of prefabricated houses in Ilijaš. Pensioner. Father of three children: Spomenka, Jadranka and Radmilo. Lived in settlement Maurovići II. Peaceful and righteous man. Died on September 2, 1992, as consequence of blows to the head that had been dealt by Mustafa Dedić, nicknamed Muste, in the Health Center in Visoko on August 31, 1992.

4. Trifko Glišić (son of Dušan) (born: 1935) Pensioner. Lived in the village Kalotići with his wife and two daughters, Snezana and Biljana. Pleasant person and good neighbour. Pensioned forest ranger, previously employed at the company Šumarstvo, Vareš. Killed by shell explosion in room No. 4, on September 25, 1992.

5. Slobodan Gogić (born: 1932) Lived in settlement Tušnjići, township Visoko. Pensioned driver. Father of two children. He was a great Serb and that cost him his life. Arrested on July 4, 1992. He succumbed to the wounds. The prison warden beat him the most.

6. Vlajko "Komljen" Samardžić (born: 1934) Lived in the village Gorani, township Visoko. Father of two sons: Srpko and Komljen. Employed at the company KTK Visoko. Serious tuberculosis patient. Died in the camp Visoko due to shortage of medicine and medical help.

7. Milutin Lukić (birthdate unknown) Lived in the settlement Zbilje, township Visoko. Worker and father of two sons: Željko and Branislav. They were also imprisoned in the camp Visoko. He was imprisoned in the weekend cottage with other Serbs from Zbilje, where they were tortured. Killed in the houseyard on September 13, 1992.

8. Svetomir Vujisić (son of Boriša) (born: March 15, 1947) Husband of Tomko Vujisić. Economist at Agro-coop Enterprise. Killed June 6 1992.

9. Stojan Gavrić - No information

10. Nikola Paradžina - No information

B. List of Prison Guards

1. Zijad Kadrić, nicknamed "Zijo"—camp warden
2. Smajlović, Kemal—camp warden
3. Burko, Šačir—shift leader
4. Burko, Suljo—shift leader
5. Kulović, Besim—shift leader
6. Kadrić, Sead, nicknamed "Šicko"—shift leader
7. Ahmić, Elmedin, nicknamed "Alme"—guard
8. Čizmić, Hasan, nicknamed "Haso"—guard
9. Dizdar, Namik—guard
10. Genjac, Eso–guard
11. Genjac, nicknamed "Pinć"—guard
12. Biogradlija, Nazif—guard
13. Ohran—guard
14. Halilović, nicknamed "Came"—guard
15. Enver, nicknamed "Keba"—guard
16. Sejdić, Jasmin—guard
17. Dedić, Muhamed, nicknamed "Gundo"—guard
18. Dedić, Edin—guard
19. Dedić, Senad—guard
20. Zukić, Muhamed—guard
21. Planinčić, Muhamed—guard
22. Lopo, Nezir—prison warden
23. Fejzic, nicknamed "Daidža"—guard
24. Hozo, Aladin from Livno—1st camp warden

C. List of Guards Who Tortured the Prisoners

1. Halilović, Hajrudin, nicknamed "Mrčo"
2. Hamzić, Asim
3. Murtić, Amir
4. Čengić, Miralem
5. Selimović, Samir, nicknamed "Domac"
6. Pulić, Esnaf, nicknamed "Esno"
7. Cikota

8. "Kengur"

Visit www.brandylanepublishers.com for a list of prisoners at Visoko.

www.ingramcontent.com/pod-product-compliance
Lightning Source LLC
Chambersburg PA
CBHW031843090426
42741CB00005B/337